SAVING THE FAMILY

LEO PATALINGHUG

SAVING
— THE —
FAMILY

THE TRANSFORMATIVE POWER OF
SHARING MEALS WITH PEOPLE YOU LOVE

SOPHIA INSTITUTE PRESS
Manchester, New Hampshire

Sophia Institute Press
Box 5284, Manchester, NH 03108
1-800-888-9344

www.SophiaInstitute.com

Sophia Institute Press® is a registered trademark of Sophia Institute.

Library of Congress Cataloging-in-Publication Data

Names: Patalinghug, Leo E., author.
Title: Saving the family : the transformative power of sharing meals with the
    people you love / Fr. Leo Patalinghug.
Description: Manchester, New Hampshire : Sophia Institute Press, [2019] |
    Includes bibliographical references.
Identifiers: LCCN 2019000542 | ISBN 9781622828180 (pbk. : alk. paper)
Subjects: LCSH: Food. | Intergenerational relations. | Families.
Classification: LCC GN407 .P38 2019 | DDC 305.2 — dc23 LC record available at https://lccn.loc.gov/2019000542

First printing

This book is dedicated to my family, imperfect as we are.
We are trying to be faithful to each other so that we can
more genuinely celebrate our human family and
can one day, if we're "Plating Grace,"
celebrate with our Heavenly Family.

RECIPE INDEX

CONTENTS

RECIPE INDEX

PREFACE

My work with families began in the 1990s, when I started my process to become a priest in Baltimore, Maryland. I spent years helping young adults grapple with life's most challenging issues, while providing premarital counseling and spiritual guidance to other parishioners.

As a third-degree black belt and former break dancer, I was able to *break down* a lot of barriers with the teens at my parish. Calling on my culinary training from my time in the seminary in Rome, I also *broke* bread with as many families as possible. I sat with families in their grief and celebrated with them in their joy, ultimately gaining lifetimes of experience from hundreds of families.

Over the years, I have been humbled and amazed to discover how universal our struggles can be. With 40 percent of Americans working more than fifty hours a week[1] and the majority of households with two working parents,[2] everyone is struggling to make time for what is important. And yet, even though we are working more, money is still tight, with nearly 40 percent of American households in debt.[3]

Growing up, my own family faced many of these same difficulties. My father often had to work late, which put a lot of pressure on my mother to keep up with me and my three siblings. As immigrants, my parents were also living hundreds of miles away from their support system.

Despite these challenges, my parents were able to create and maintain a strong, loving, supportive family. Later, as I began working with families around the world, I met many people who overcame even greater obstacles to build happy, healthy families. Longing to share the source of these families' strength with others, I began to investigate what they had in common.

The answer was almost shocking in its simplicity: regular family meals.

---

[1] Chris Isidore and Tami Luhby, "Turns Out Americans Work Really Hard ... but Some Want to Work Harder," CNN, July 9, 2015, https://money.cnn.com/2015/07/09/news/economy/americans-work-bush/.

[2] Bureau of Labor Statistics, *Employment Characteristics of Families Summary*, April 19, 2018, https://www.bls.gov/news.release/famee.nr0.htm.

[3] *Average Credit Card Debt in America: January 2019*, Value Penguin, https://www.valuepenguin.com/average-credit-card-debt.

Now, family mealtime may sound like a leftover relic from the *Leave It to Beaver* days of long ago, but there is hard data to support my family-meal theory. Regular family meals are proven to do the following:

- *Increase academic performance*: kids on average have 38 percent better grades.[4]
- *Improve communication*: kids are 40 percent more likely to tell parents about their problems.[5]
- *Lower high-risk behaviors*: kids are less likely to smoke, drink, and use drugs.[6]
- *Cultivate healthy eating habits*: kids are 40 percent less likely to be overweight.[7]
- *Improve emotional well-being*: kids experience lower levels of depression.[8]

My formal quest to help families grow stronger through regular meals began in earnest in 2002 with the founding of Grace Before Meals,[9] now known as Plating Grace. What started as an idea transformed into a full-fledged international movement with books, a TV show, and more—all centered on the dinner table. Today, I am blessed to be able to speak with families around the world, presenting and cooking for all types of people while continuing to learn from them.

What my work with connecting food and faith has taught me is that while family meals can sound like a simple solution, carving out time to eat together every day is extremely difficult for modern families. And yet there are ways to fit regular meals into our fast-paced lives. Although families' methods are different, in sifting through them all, I've discovered certain foundational principals that can be applied by any family.

As a professional cook, I thought about presenting this information like a recipe—a list of ingredients with simple steps to follow so that every family can benefit from the ritual of eating regular meals together. But although I love simple, succinct steps for recreating a delicious meal, I've come to respect the fact that families are more intricate than even the most temperamental

---

[4] National Center for Addiction and Substance Abuse at Columbia University, *The Importance of Family Meals IV* (New York: National Center for Addiction and Substance Abuse, 2007).

[5] Ibid.

[6] Ibid.

[7] Cody C. Delistraty, "The Importance of Eating Together," *Atlantic*, July 8, 2014, https://www.theatlantic.com/health/archive/2014/07/the-importance-of-eating-together/374256/.

[8] Frank J. Elgar, Wendy Craig, and Stephen J. Trites, "Family Dinners, Communication, and Mental Health in Canadian Adolescents," *Journal of Adolescent Health* 52, no. 4 (April 2013): 433–438, https://www.jahonline.org/article/S1054-139X(12)00317-5/fulltext.

[9] I evolved the name in order to reach out beyond the Church. To me it was more of a movement than a "ministry" only for religious people. I want to acknowledge and thank the Team of Renegade Productions for helping to get Grace Before Meals off the ground and for the support in coordinating the production of this book.

soufflé. Only those in the family can truly understand what makes it tick, and only the heads of the household are properly equipped to ensure that the whole thing doesn't cave in.

So, instead of a recipe, I've pulled together a series of practical tips and real-world exercises that will help you become what I am calling your family's "Supper" Hero. Raising a family is a serious responsibility, and feeding your family what they need—whether that's discipline, gratitude, or understanding—calls for superhero-like qualities.

Each chapter of this book is designed to explore critical insights I've gleaned from working with families around the world. There are also exercises inspired by families I've met to guide you along the way. In addition, I've included some great recipes you can enjoy with your family to make sure you aren't just "feeding" them metaphorically.[10]

Through fun, practical exercises and conversation starters, I hope to help you move toward your goals for a healthier family life. I'm excited to help you strengthen the traits that make your family special and help you grow even stronger in the years to come. And I am excited to continue to learn and grow with you. I hope this is only the first edition, with many more insights from families like yours to come.

---

[10] These recipes are twice tested, by families and by Chef Keith Holsey. I want to thank those families and Chef Keith for making sure these recipes are simply doable and simply delicious!

SAVING THE FAMILY

THE SUPPER HERO'S MISSION

Why Our Families Need Regular Meals

Did you know that the average American family spends only eight hours together each week—and just thirty-six minutes each day between Monday and Friday?[11] It's true! And with the majority of American households made up of two working parents, at least 40 percent of whom work more than fifty hours a week, it's not hard to see why this happens.

Families are battling the demanding realities of our modern lives in different ways and with different effects. But too many people I talk to are getting swept up in a wave of hopelessness. They also are getting so caught up in their role as provider that they let their other important roles (nurturer, protector, and mentor) take a backseat.

---

[11] Jaymi McCann, "No Time for the Family? You Are Not Alone: Parents and Children Spend Less Than an Hour with Each Other Every Day Because of Modern Demands," *Daily Mail*, July 14, 2013, https://www.dailymail.co.uk/news/article-2363193/No-time-family-You-Parents-children-spend-hour-day-modern-demands.html.

Top 5 Reasons for Not Getting Enough Family Time[12]

1. Work	3. School/Homework	5. Extracurricular
2. Chores	4. TV/Screen Time	Activities

Many families end up feeling like the average hour a day together in front of the TV (60 percent of families spend their time together this way)[13] is really the best they can do. But as I see it, there are three choices we all have as the hectic world begins spinning out of control around us: (1) We can be victims; (2) we can be villains; or (3) we can be what our families really need.

Introducing the Supper Hero

You may be thinking, "Father Leo, the choice between victims, villains, and heroes is pretty limiting. It would work only if every scenario in life involved a set of train tracks and Dudley Do-Right. The real world is more complicated, with more gray areas"—but I don't think it is.

People who let their challenges run their lives are victims. Those who stand in the way of someone else's growth are villains. And the ones who take a stand against the societal forces tearing our families apart, those, ladies and gentlemen, are our supper heroes.

This book is all about how anyone can be the supper hero in his family's life. So, what exactly is a supper hero? Well, in addition to being a very well-thought-out pun, a supper hero is the term I use to describe the countless parents I've met around the world who are helping their family grow stronger together, through good times and bad.

In this book, supper hero can refer to a singular hero, a dynamic duo, or a larger support system dedicated to helping form the family. Families come in all shapes and sizes, but anyone who has taken on the tremendous task of raising a family has the opportunity to be a supper hero.

---

[12] Rick Maughan, "Parents 'Spend Just 34 Minutes a Day with Their Children'—Because Stressful Life Is Too Distracting," *Mirror*, April 14, 2015, https://www.mirror.co.uk/news/uk-news/parents-spend-just-34-minutes-5518081.

[13] Maughan, "Just 34 Minutes."

What Does a Supper Hero Do?

Supper heroes tackle head-on the problems facing modern families. Instead of getting swept up in negativity, they search for the bright side. They set realistic expectations and find time for their family, even when there seems to be none.

Supper heroes don't look for the quick fix or the easy route. They ask for the patience and the guidance to take the right path. In going against the grain and standing up for what is right, supper heroes set their family up for success. They give their family the right tools so that they can learn and grow through whatever life throws their way.

Supper heroes do more than provide for their families. They nurture, protect, guide, teach, and support in order to help their family thrive. They provide the formation needed to transform their family members into the superheroes our world needs.

FOOD FOR THOUGHT

What Is Your Role?

My concept of the family supper hero stems from my experience in seminary working with a faith formation director. We called him our *formator* because he helped "form" us into our roles as faith leaders.

When I talk about a supper hero, I am talking about a "family formation director"—anyone responsible for the formation of a family, as my faith formation director was responsible for my formation as a Catholic priest.

Anatomy of a Supper Hero

Just like the heroes in movies, supper heroes come in all shapes and sizes, but here is a quick outline of what it takes to be a supper hero:

A Grateful Heart

Our society has a bias toward negativity. We tend to see only the negatives in our lives and only the faults in ourselves and others. Although supper heroes have bad days and tough times, they don't let life's setbacks or their own shortcomings define them. They have a grateful heart. Even in the worst of times, they are able to look at their lives, seeing the good and the bad, and smile.

Clear Eyes

When things don't go our way, we get disappointed. I've spoken with many people who try to take on more than their family can handle or want something out of life that just

Every Family Has Their Own "Regular"

Lots of parents come to me with what they think is a unique reason why their family can't have regular meals together. I like to use my brother as an example of how any family can make it happen. My brother and his family teach karate every day until 9:00 p.m., leaving no time for regular family meals, right? Wrong! They eat a small snack earlier in the day but then eat a moderate dinner together every night at 10:00 p.m. after closing up the school. They developed a routine. It may not be traditional, but it's their "regular."

isn't in the cards. They are discontented because they want the moon! Heroes dream with their eyes wide open. They set realistic expectations and take pride in what they achieve as a family, instead of focusing on what they may never have.

Open Arms

Getting caught up in the pressures of modern life can pull us in a million directions. We end up growing apart and consequently don't know how to turn to each other when important issues arise. Supper heroes know they can't do it alone. They work on growing together as a family every day so they are prepared for whatever lies ahead.

A Questioning Mind

It's hard to take a deeper look at life's most challenging questions. Many people stay on the surface, where everything is easy and safe. Heroes make time to reflect on the world around them and ask themselves the big questions. In digging into deeper issues, they get a better understanding of themselves and what they want for their family.

Patience

Our culture demands instant gratification. We want the quick fix, the fast solution. But the work of relationship building is never done—ever. A supper hero understands that a healthy family takes years of hard work and that even the strongest families require daily attention.

What Is a "Healthy" Family?

We all have our own concepts of what a healthy family is and our own goals for what we want for our families. In this book, when I talk about healthy families, I'm talking about families that:

- understand their own struggles
- come together to overcome difficulties
- live healthy lifestyles
- make good decisions
- experience joy and hope despite challenges
- know how to argue appropriately
- say "I'm sorry"
- hold strong beliefs

❷ **DID YOU KNOW?** Americans have a negativity bias. According to a 2016 study by the American Council on Science and Health, only 6 percent of Americans believe that the world is getting better.[14] I firmly believe this negativity is poison to a happy, healthy family life. It lies to us, telling us that our family problems are insurmountable mountains instead of mere speed bumps that God has put in our way for a reason.

The Supper Hero's Mission

Remember that show *Heroes*? Its advertising slogan was everywhere: "Save the cheerleader, save the world." Now, I don't know exactly how she saved the world, I'm not that far into my Netflix queue. But the line always stuck with me because I believe we can all be heroes, and I believe we can all do something small that will ultimately help make the world a better place. No, not saving the cheerleader. Saving the family meal!

Although every family faces its own unique challenges, a universal goal we all have is keeping our families together. And while carving out time in your life for sit-down family dinners may seem like a herculean task, it will make creating a strong, happy family much easier.

---

[14] Alex Berezow, "Only 6% of Americans Think the World Is Getting Better," American Council on Science and Health, July 3, 2016, https://www.acsh.org/news/2016/07/03/only-6-of-americans-think-world-is-getting-better.

Never Too Late

I once spoke with a divorced man who began dating a woman with young kids. He hadn't had regular meals with his own children, but he wanted to do so after experiencing family dinners with his new girlfriend and her family. Although he couldn't go back in time, he was able to start regular monthly meals with his own children.

We Choose Our Own Futures

I'd like to share a quote, attributed to Oscar Wilde, that helps me tremendously. He said, "Every saint has a past. Every sinner has a future."

Before I became a priest, I thought about leaving priestly formation. I didn't think I would be a good priest because I wasn't a "perfect" candidate with a perfect past. But this quote helps capture a truth: that my future could be anything I chose. I also was inspired by historical figures such as St. Augustine, who turned away from a worldly lifestyle after many years to become a saint.

I picked the future I wanted, and you can do the same for your family.

When it comes to the slow process of building a strong family, our need for instant gratification often works against us. Your goal as a supper hero is to establish the ritual of family meals in your household. This can be challenging, but regular meals build into your life the time you need to dedicate to your family. You end up growing together, meal by meal.

Will You Go on This Quest?

In every hero's tale, there is a moment when the hero can choose to accept the challenge and go on the adventure or to stay home. For you, this is that moment. And yes, your hero's challenge has been issued by a third-degree black belt, break-dancing, award-winning cook — and, oh yeah, a priest too.

You are being challenged to dig deep and really explore what family means to you, to examine your perception and perhaps change your perspective. But as harrowing as all this may seem, know that the wisdom of hundreds of families from around the world is right here in these pages to guide you. I am also here to offer insights into different methods that have helped countless families.

As a cook, I've always found it amazing how the addition of a single ingredient can change an entire recipe. Introducing salt to a stew, for example, can draw out and deepen flavors. These pages will help you to become the salt in any of your relationships — and not in the "salt in the wound" kind of way.

Raising a family is the ultimate quest. It's like a long, slow Crock-Pot recipe — well worth the time and effort! If you are ready to accept this important mission and have regular family meals with your family, then let's get to it!

> ❷ **DID YOU KNOW?** Family meals are rare. Less than 30 percent of families make the time to eat together every day.[15]

EXERCISES

1. Keep track of where your time goes.

   Every family has different conflicts that seem to get in the way of family time. Pinpointing your obstacles is the first step to coming up with a solution to overcome them. I suggest that you chart out your week. Think about the things that could end up competing with regular meals in your house. There will be circumstances you have control over and some that you have to work around. In the upcoming chapters, we'll dive into strategies for both. But keeping these things in mind will be helpful.

2. Consider what a healthy family looks like to you.

   In this chapter, we talked a little bit about what a healthy family looks like, but we all have our own concepts of what a healthy family is. Review this part of the chapter, and reflect on what you want for your own family.

3. Pay attention to your strengths and weaknesses.

   Being a superhero is a lot to live up to. It's impossible, day in and day out, to be all of the things outlined in this chapter. We're only human, after all. The point is to realize what you need to be doing for your family so you can work toward that ideal. This week, pay attention to the areas in which you are strongest and the areas in which you are weakest. As you read the family stories throughout this book, note what others have done in areas of weakness.

---

[15] "Youth Statistics: Family Structure and Relationships," Act for Youth, http://www.actforyouth.net/adolescence/demographics/family.cfm./

4. Use a comfort meal to create a comfortable atmosphere for a discussion.

Should you accept this mission, here's a recipe for you to digest: Crock-Pot Macaroni and Cheese. It's a family-tested, family-friendly menu to help you discuss these concepts with your family around a dinner table. Turn to page 109 for the recipe.

WHO'S ON YOUR TEAM?

Exploring Your Family's Dynamics

Master chefs can use any combination of ingredients because they know how to complement each distinct flavor without overpowering, distracting or destroying the unique quality of the others—which is exactly what parents have to do!

It is no easy task, and it can be especially challenging when our family is a basket of mystery ingredients. Those of us who have grown distant from a family member or have a teenager who is pulling away really have to step up our game. It's up to us to learn about our family "ingredients" so we can bring everyone together in the one balanced "dish" that we call family.

But while you are like a chef trying to create the perfect bite, it's important to remember that this isn't *Hell's Kitchen* and you aren't Gordon Ramsay. Your goal isn't to force your family to meet your desired outcome. In cooking, processing things too much renders them inedible. The same is true with families. Instead of overmolding your family into something it's not, supper heroes learn to play to everyone's strengths.

Being the Good Kind of Tool

The secret is humility. Many people hear the word *humility* and think *humiliation*, but that isn't what we are talking about here. *Humility* is defined as not haughty or arrogant. To be humble, it might be helpful to think of yourself as the tools used in the kitchen — instead of as the chef.

Tools, like supper heroes, serve more than one purpose. For example, a knife's blade is its most popular feature, but its blunt end is needed to cut open a coconut. Similarly, you are the provider for your family, but that's not your only role. You are also the nurturer, counselor, protector, and more — when you need to be.

Like the chef who has to try over and over again to get the perfect bite, we have to experiment to see how everyone can best fit together. Creating a happy family isn't the same as ordering fast food, after all. It's a long-term Crock-Pot adventure.

What's in Your Cupboard?

Before trying to create your family "meal," take inventory and see what ingredients you have to work with. You may be surprised by what you discover. For example, my twin niece and nephew have many things in common, but their personalities are completely different! And I have to treat them each a little differently to accommodate their opposite natures.

To understand the variety and flavors of life in a family, we need to learn about the various characteristics that make up a person's personality. Each of these temperaments requires patient study, the way chefs study the reactions and various anatomies of their ingredients.

►€ FOOD FOR THOUGHT
The Power of Humility

Researchers from the University of Chicago are studying humility's impact on close social relationships.* Initial evidence supports the theory that humility increases commitment in relationships. Research has also shown that by letting go of the need to control, participants lead less stressful lives, which leads to improved health.

* Don Emerson Davis Jr. and Joshua N. Hook, "Measuring Humility and Its Positive Effects," Center for Practical Wisdom, posted December 10, 2013, http://wisdomresearch.org/blogs/news/archive/2013/12/10/measuring-humility-and-its-positive-effects.aspx.

Temperaments are generic categories that explain how certain types of people generally approach situations or relationships. They also determine what a person's "temperature" is when confronting various experiences. Each temperament describes two sides of the same coin, and it's often easy to see which side a person uses most often.

- A *choleric* person is a leader who is good at making decisions and finding solutions and who can also be irritable and quick tempered (burning-high heat).
- A *sanguine* person is an optimistic social butterfly who can also be a bit pushy and controlling (medium-high heat).
- A *melancholic* person has a quiet, analytical mind and can tend to be shy and to be overlooked (medium heat).
- A *phlegmatic* person is a relaxed, peaceful individual who is not easily motivated and can be lazy (low heat).

> ❷ **DID YOU KNOW?** Greeks are known for more than yogurt. The concept of temperaments comes from ancient Greek society, where doctors understood health by examining a person's temperament—the "temperature" of his personality. Philosophers later began to use this system as well, describing the four temperaments.

Your Family's Flavor Profile

From a foodie's perspective, I love the idea of people operating at different temperatures. As we handle different ingredients at different temperatures, we have to use different levels of intensity when handling different temperaments!

We can also think of temperaments as flavors—and not only because some temperaments are harder for me to digest than others! By thinking of the temperaments from a culinary perspective, it's easy to see how each temperament relates to and reacts with the others.

The Sanguine Person: A Salty Sea Dog

To me, a sanguine personality can be thought of like salt. Salty foods are great to chill out a sour taste, as sanguine people are great at balancing out sour or phlegmatic temperaments. Salt is also needed to bring out the flavors of other ingredients, but it should be used sparingly. Likewise, sanguine personalities are great at socializing and drawing others out of their shells, but they shouldn't go so far as to force family members into doing things they don't want to do.

The Choleric Person: A Bitter Pill to Swallow

Choleric personalities are like a bitter flavor. But while their quick tempers can be difficult to handle, that is only one aspect of their personality. It's important to remember that bitter foods also have healing properties and antioxidants. Likewise, choleric personalities can be just what a family needs to make important decisions. Bitter flavors are balanced out by sweetness. That's why a choleric person's ability to make decisions is strengthened by a melancholy person's ability to analyze situations.

The Melancholic Person: The Sweet Tooth

A melancholic temperament is just like the sweet flavor — easy to digest until it becomes a cavity creator! The melancholic's analytical mind and quiet nature can make him an easygoing family member, but it's important not to overlook him. In the culinary world, a bitter flavor is balanced by adding sweet. Therefore, add a melancholic personality to the short-fuse choleric personality, and you'll see the two even each other out.

The Phlegmatic Person: Sour Pucker Face

A phlegmatic person might be compared to a sour flavor, which can mute strong flavors. That is why I love using lemon to balance out seafood dishes with bitter greens. A phlegmatic person is relaxed and peaceful but can also be laid back to the point of laziness. Here, a sanguine personality can provide the perfect balance. A sanguine person's optimism and energy can be just what a phlegmatic person needs to avoid chilling out into an immobile sloth.

What's Your Recipe?

At this point, you're probably wondering which one of these temperaments describes you to a T, or maybe you're surprised to find that you're a little bit of each. That's okay! The study of temperaments isn't about finding a box that we fit into perfectly. It's about observing and understanding our natural tendencies and the typical approach we have when things heat up in the "kitchen of life."

Temperaments help us understand how our differences fit together. Knowing the strengths and weaknesses of each family member can help us relate and build each other up as well as communicate better and work through difficult challenges as a team. With humble efforts of trial and error and the indomitable spirit of a life learner, you and your family can be the masterpiece of goodness and harmony that this world is hungering for.

EXERCISES

1. Become more aware of your family members' temperaments.

    It's important to start from a place of self-knowledge and acceptance. In understanding your own strengths and weaknesses, it's easier to see the positives and negatives that each of your family members brings to the table. Remember, you are seeking to understand, not to judge. You may have a quick temper or a tendency to procrastinate, but that isn't bad! You just have to learn to play to your strengths—to balance those aspects for the benefit of your family.

2. Explore our larger human family.

    I firmly believe we are all part of one big human family. Use family meals as an opportunity to explore our human family by trying different food and different flavors from around the world. You can pick any culture you want to discuss and then find a relevant dish, or vice versa. This food adventure can help keep dinnertime fresh!

3. Use your powers for good, not evil.

    This chapter may have opened your eyes to how your family operates, or you may have already been aware of exactly what makes your family members tick. Either way, it's important to use this insightful information for good, not for evil. In other words, don't use what you know about how your family members operate to help you persuade them to do what you want them to. It can be a fine line to walk between parenting and control. Examine how you use your insights when it comes to interacting with your family.

4. Test how well your family members know each other's "flavors."

    Put your family members' names into a hat, and have each person draw a name. Then, everyone should use what he knows to create the perfect skewer for the person whose name he picked. See the recipe on page 110.

YOUR SUPPER HERO POWER

Knowing What to Feed Your Family

———

Have you noticed how superheroes all have a wise mentor who guides them along the way? This sage character sees something in them that no one else does and proceeds to teach them how to be an amazing martial artist, gymnast, basket weaver, or what-have-you in one high-octane training montage until, one day, the hero student "becomes the master."

Well, while I *do* have years of experience counseling families and a black belt in Tae Kwon Do, I hope it doesn't disappoint you to learn I am not going to be your wise old mentor. Not only am I not "that old," but if my work with families across the globe has taught me anything, it's that as an outsider, I will never know the members of your family or your goals as intimately as you do.

This insight is your supper-hero super power. Like many heroes, you may not have realized that you had this power inside you. And you may not be able to harness it right away. That's okay. As with everything worthwhile, becoming the supper hero for your family takes time, practice, and perspective.

Where I Come In

Instead of acting as your wise, old mentor, I am here to challenge your perceptions of what is achievable. You may be short on time and energy during the week, but it's the quality of time you spend together as a family, not the quantity. There are ways to maximize what you have to grow together as a family.

In providing an examination of how other families are making regular meals work for them, I will help you, or you and your spouse, determine what will work best for your family. In challenging your perceptions of what is achievable, I will help you see outside your limits to the opportunities you have.

We will be diving into a step-by-step method for getting started with family meals, but before we do, it's important to reflect on what you want to feed them when you get them around the dinner table.

More Than Just Food

I'm sure you're familiar with the Food Pyramid. Everything we need to eat daily is at the bottom—grains, fruits, and vegetables—and what we all ultimately want to eat is at the top—sugary sweet deliciousness. But when it comes to meeting our other needs, it's a different bottom-up-style pyramid we should turn to.

In 1943, Abraham Maslow developed a leveled pyramid to describe what human beings need in order to attain fulfillment. In Maslow's hierarchy of needs, food, water, and air are at the bottom. They are what we need in order to survive. Once this basic level is met, the next thing we need as humans is security. After that, we reach the level of love and belonging and then work to attain esteem. All of these levels build to the top of the pyramid, Maslow's equivalent of the Girl Scout Thin Mint Cookie, self-actualization.

Maslow's hierarchy is just one way to think about our human needs, but it's very helpful in organizing the way

FATS, OILS, AND SWEETS
Use sparingly

MILK, YOGURT, AND CHEESE
2 to 3 servings

MEATS, BEANS, EGGS, AND NUTS
2 to 3 servings

VEGETABLES
3 to 5 servings

FRUITS
2 to 4 servings

BREAD, CEREAL, RICE, AND PASTA
6 to 11 servings

we think about what we need to "feed" our family. In looking at Maslow's pyramid we see that while physiological needs such as food are very important, we all have more than just dietary needs that have to be met.

It's easy to become so focused on providing the basic needs of food and security for our family that we don't consider the other levels of the pyramid. As a result, we start to hunger for something more, often without true knowledge of what we are searching for. This adds to our feeling of being lost, of being a victim. It can also lead us to overindulge in eating, drinking, and other unhealthy behaviors to fill the void.

I've found the best way to satisfy Maslow's pyramid while staying balanced and healthy is with my favorite four-letter *F* word of all time—*F.O.O.D.* I'm not just talking about what satisfies our bellies. I'm talking about something deeper—something that all families are craving even if they don't know it. I'm talking about: Fidelity, Obedience, Opportunity and Discernment.

Try This *F* Word on for Size: <u>Fidelity</u>

SELF-ACTUALIZATION
Achieving one's full potential

ESTEEM NEEDS
Prestige and feelings of accomplishment

BELONGINGNESS AND LOVE NEEDS
Intimate relationships, friends

SAFTEY NEEDS
Security, safety

PHYSIOLOGICAL NEEDS
Food, water, warmth, rest

Fidelity is not an easy word to understand, and it is much more difficult to fulfill. At a basic level, it is faithfulness to a person demonstrated by continued loyalty and support. These concepts of fidelity and faith go beyond an affiliation with a religious organization (though, as a priest, I can tell you that religion isn't a bad place to start). When you demonstrate fidelity, you are showing your commitment to the people important to you. Fidelity basically says, "No matter what, I'll always be there!"

Even when we can't physically be around for another person, an attitude of fidelity assures our loved ones that they are not alone. In good times and bad, health and sickness, wealth and poverty, we are committed to being there for them. That is what fidelity for our family means. And it's this security that so many families hunger for. How we show our families fidelity is by feeding them—body, mind, and spirit.

Experiencing Fidelity

When my dad was recovering from back surgery, I had the privilege of spending time caring for him. It was a trying time. There was the anxiety-ridden surgery, the late nights comforting loved ones, the high medical bills, and the long, painful recovery.

Instead of letting that negative voice talk to me, I saw the whole experience as an opportunity to savor the good things. And as I carefully spoon-fed oatmeal to my father, I realized that I was giving him much more than daily sustenance. What I was really feeding him was my fidelity.

Because I Said So: Obedience

Parents want obedient children. That typically means that they want their offspring to comply with their laws and to respect their authority. Under this definition of obedience, "Because I said so" becomes a perfectly reasonable law of the land. But the word *obedience* doesn't come from the Latin word for "martial law." It comes from the Latin word for "to listen." So, when we talk about obedience as it relates to family, we're talking about a spiritual sustenance we all crave. We all long to be heard. And we know how unsatisfying it is when people don't listen.

Listening can be a struggle in today's device-filled world. In order to listen to another person, you have to step away not only from distractions but also from your own thoughts and opinions. Family dinners are a great time for families to obey each other by listening.

Cookie-Cutter Children

A mother was struggling with disobedient children. In talking with her, I saw that she was so focused on getting them to do what she wanted that she wasn't listening to why they weren't doing what she said. She and I talked about obedience as listening, and she agreed to shift her focus to listening more.

When I met up with her again, she shared that she realized that some of the things she wanted her children to do were unrealistic. There wasn't enough time for them to do all their homework and chores before dinner, for example. They weren't disobeying as much as choosing their own priorities. After listening to each other, the family came up with a solution that worked for everyone.

Don't Miss Out: <u>Opportunity</u>

While sports, dance class, community theater, and other activities are good chances for families to get together, you'll want to create family opportunities in which you aren't a spectator, or worse, a chauffeur. Mealtime is a perfect opportunity for family interaction and togetherness. But it's important that we don't let the consistency of a daily meal give way to monotony. This sameness is the gateway to boredom, apathy, and disengagement. And we don't want to create an *opportunity* for our family to disengage. Instead, we need to make moments of discovery, wonder, and awe for our families by seeking out new experiences.

Opportunity is a gift you can share with your family, but the simple act of trying new things also teaches your family members to do the same. This makes opportunity the daily bread that sustains our loved ones for their entire lives. It is the food that keeps on feeding!

There are also many nurturing opportunities to feed your family through the difficulties and challenges of life. Seasons of hardship, sickness, and financial insecurity are not a curse but are incredible opportunities to learn gratitude, compassion, and faith.

> ❓ **DID YOU KNOW?** There is opportunity in crisis. In Chinese, *crisis* has a secondary meaning, "opportunity." These concepts are two sides of the same coin.

Did I Do That? <u>Discernment</u>

Of all of the foods that families feed each other, discernment, to me, is the most important. Without it, families are unable to make key decisions.

According to the *Oxford Living Dictionary*, *discernment* means "the ability to judge well." From its Latin origin, it implies the thoughtful art of making distinctions. It also relates to the act of sifting. As the baker sifts flour, we too must sift through all the possibilities in life to discern the proper path to take.

Identifying what is important is a challenge, because it means facing conflicting viewpoints and ruling out other possible avenues. It's much easier to operate on the surface, rather than having to dig deeper to get through our day-to-day challenges. But digging deep is important work.

Many of the families I work with use family meals as *the* time to discern together. They incorporate the act of "sifting" through their lives as a daily practice. In feeding each other a regular portion of discernment, they begin to see one another's true value and to have more confidence when discerning the best decisions to make in their lives together.

You Are Ready

So far, we've explored why your family needs a supper hero, what a supper hero does, and how being the supper hero for your family can help you all become stronger and healthier together. We've also considered the personalities of your family members and considered what they need to be fed.

If this were a recipe, we'd have already gathered our ingredients, skimmed ahead, seen what skills were needed to create the dish—maybe even preheated the oven. The point is, we'd be ready to go step by step through the recipe to create the meal. But that's not how being a supper hero works.

The best meals on earth happen when chefs make them their own. Similarly, you have to take ownership of your family. But unlike with recipes, just because you determine the best way to help your children today, that doesn't mean the same system will work for them as they age. But don't worry. While you need to search within yourself for the answers, I will be here every step of the way.

What are you waiting for? Let's get this dinner party started.

EXERCISES

1. Practice fidelity.

    Always being there for those you care about doesn't just mean being there physically. Think about some ways you can show your family that you will be there for them no matter what!

2. Practice obedience.

    A good listener doesn't finish sentences or try to "fix" problems. Bring this approach into your mealtime conversations. Exercise patience and a good ear so that you will really hear your family. Keep note of things you wanted to say but refrained from saying in order to let your family members speak. Then look back at those things later and discern whether they really needed to be said.

3. Take an opportunity to mix it up!

    Monotony can cause family members to want to disengage from mealtime. Try to keep things fresh by introducing meals from around the world. Start by having one global dinner a month. Talk about the culture, the people, and the ambiance around a thematic dinner.

4. Think about what you're grateful for.

Discernment helps each person to be aware of, and hopefully grateful for, the other members of the family. Make a list of all the things you are grateful for in each member of your family, and try using this list as a conversation starter during your next family meal. Get them thinking about all the things they're grateful for.

5. Practice discernment and obedience in the kitchen.

Make East and West Pasta, two distinct dishes that use the same pound of spaghetti and that are both *faithful* to the spaghetti noodle. They are two dishes I've *discerned* to give you the *opportunity* to be *obedient* to your family's request for pasta night! See the recipes on pages 112 and 113.

YOUR TRAINING BEGINS

Getting Started with Regular Meals

Riding a bike starts with taking off the training wheels; learning to high-dive begins with that first plunge. Having regular family meals is no different. We just have to get up the courage to go for it! Then, of course, we must develop the discipline to pick ourselves back up and try again if we get a skinned knee or perform some kind of miraculously painful belly flop.

If you are feeling like that kid up there ready to do a high dive, it's okay. Launching into anything new invites a fear of the unknown, along with doubts and anxieties. And these feelings can be compounded if your kids are older and no longer as obedient as dependent toddlers.

But although being apprehensive is understandable, you can't let it become an excuse to delay or avoid broaching the subject at all. Do you really have to wait until the summer holiday, or until the kids go back to school, or well, until whatever reason you may have for not starting family meals *this week* or *tonight*?

Imagine if a superhero acted with the same hesitation and fear. The world (and our families) would be victims without hope. There will be setbacks as you begin this process and maybe even some discouraging moments or hurt feelings. But remember, regular family meals are integral to a healthy family life. In the end, the benefits make it worth getting out of your comfort zone.

Still not ready to take the plunge? Well, how 'bout a little faith and encouragement? I promise you will not sink. I may be pushing you toward a precipice, but believe me, it's only because I know you can do this. You *can* develop regular, intentional family meals — even if it begins with a terrifying leap and a little kicking and screaming.

How do I know this? Well, there are certain fundamental mechanics I've seen families all over the world put into place to build regular family meals. Whether you have teenagers or adult children with families of their own, you can use these steps to get you started.

Step 1: Get a Meal Buddy

The good news is that, as with going to a gym, you can get support when you start having your family meals. Get a helpful meal buddy who will motivate you and serve as a sounding board or a recipe sharer, or both. This person is there to help keep you accountable to the discipline of dinnertime. And you can do the same for your meal buddy. Remember, we're in this together!

This person could be your spouse, another family member, someone from your church or neighborhood who values the importance of family meals, or even a local chef! Collaborate with this person. Exchange ideas, successes, and failures. But most of all, give each other guilt-free accountability in making this ritual a priority for each of your families.

FAMILY STORY

The Cigar Club

I know a group of meal-buddy dads who would meet to discuss cooking and family meal ideas over a couple of cigars. I call this group the Holy Smokers. They made family meal planning fun!

Step 2: Make It Regular

Allowing mealtime to be pushed aside for something else diminishes its importance. Family meals can't be abandoned just because someone is running late or something else comes up. Respect the time set aside for family meals, and keep to your schedule as much as possible.

Regularity is achievable! Even families with graveyard night shifts or on-call duty can find the time to schedule family meals with a sense of dependable consistency. The key is making regular family meals a priority. Once this critical perspective shift occurs, other things won't be able to edge out your time together, because family meals will come first.

The first step is selecting when your family meals will take place. This can seem like an impossible task, especially for those of us who have lost all control over a schedule filled to the brim with conflicting responsibilities. Work, school, rehearsals, the gym—it all seems to gobble up what little time we have. But if we don't become the masters of our schedules, they will become the masters of us.

If a nightly 5:00 or 6:00 or even 7:00 mealtime just won't work, it's okay to employ a little flexibility. Even if you're having dinner together only four nights out of the week, or even just one major dinner, the "routine" establishes the regularity that's so critical to making mealtime a priority.

If you can make it work, a nightly meal at a certain time is best. But maybe it is more realistic to schedule meals on school nights only, one weekly meal on Sunday nights, or something else. Take some time to look at your schedule and see what will work best for you. Talk with your meal buddy or someone else in your support group and settle on something that is achievable and that you can do consistently. Above all, talk with your family about when these regular meals will happen.

Out-of-the-Box Meals

Regular can mean something different for every family. Here are some out-of-the-box meals you can schedule regularly for your family:

- Afterschool snack
- Study break
- Late-night cup of tea
- Breakfast

FAMILY STORY

Digital Dining with Dad

I met a family who found a solution for how to have family dinners together even though the husband traveled a lot for work. When Dad was away, the rest of the family would gather as usual, only there would be a laptop at Dad's place. Then he Skyped into the meal! Sometimes he would even eat the same food. The kids loved it, and the parents loved that it helped them keep family meals regular.

Write down a schedule that works for you:

Sunday: _____

Monday: _____

Tuesday: _____

Wednesday: _____

Thursday: _____

Friday: _____

Saturday: _____

Step 3: Consider the Ritual

Family meals feel regular because they are held at a certain time, but they also follow a certain pattern. Maybe the family comes together to help prepare the meal or set the table. There are different rituals that show they are working together for a common goal. Each of these lets the family members lean on each other and be woven closer together. It's a natural experience of connectedness and personal investment into someone or something beyond ourselves.

There are multiple opportunities to build rituals during a family meal:

- *Before eating*, there is the opportunity to give thanks for the food and for those who helped to prepare it. Think about how you would like your family to do this. Maybe you want to pray and give thanks to God or to acknowledge the farm the food came from or the family members who helped to provide the food. A toast before the meal, even with water or milk, can serve as a powerful ritual of togetherness and goodwill. Whatever it is, think about how you want your family to express their gratitude.

- *At the table*, everyone usually sits in certain chairs. The family supper heroes may sit at the head of the table to symbolize their position, but the kids also pick their seats. In my family, we each had a place around the table. It wasn't formally given out; it was just adopted and then maintained over the years so that we grew accustomed to where everyone sat. When someone was missing, we felt the emptiness of that chair. This ritual is a powerful reminder that there is always a place at the table for you.

- *As the meal begins*, there are table manners that can be observed, which is a perfect opportunity to let your kids practice discipline. Is it important to you that the table was set correctly with knives and forks in the right place? Do you want everyone to chew with their mouths closed or to say please and thank you when passing the dishes? Think about the rules you want observed.
- *During dinner*, you have the opportunity to talk with your children. Simply asking about their day can lead to one- or two-word responses. Sharing about your own day may open the field a little bit wider. Getting your children's perspectives on current events or sharing what is important to you are possibilities. Think about what an ideal dinner conversation might be like. (Don't worry if conversations don't flow easily. I'll expand on dinner conversations in upcoming chapters.)
- *After dinner*, plates need to be cleared, dishes need to be cleaned, and countertops need to be wiped down. This is an opportunity to have your family learn the importance of contributing. Even small tasks, such as taking out the trash, make your children a part of the meal. Think about your children's ages and what they can be doing to contribute.

The ritual of the family meal helps to develop a deeper level of appreciation and intimacy for the meal you're eating and the people you are eating with.

Write down at least three rituals you would like to incorporate into family mealtime:

Before-dinner ritual: _____

During-dinner ritual: _____

After-dinner ritual: _____

> ❓ **DID YOU KNOW?** Kids want to be helpers. Young children want to create a positive identity. According to a study from the Child Development journal, young children (three- to six-year-olds) who are thanked for "being a helper" as opposed to "helping," are significantly more likely to want to lend a hand in the future.[16]

---

[16] Jennifer Breheny Wallace, "Why Children Need Chores," *Wall Street Journal*, March 13, 2015, http://www.wsj.com/articles/why-children-need-chores-1426262655.

Technology-Free Zone!

Mandating a technology-free zone lets you provide more attention to the great task at hand: feeding and nurturing your family. Putting away cell phones and turning off the TV not only helps your children to listen to you but also helps you to listen to your children.

Step 4: Take a Step Back

It's easy to get excited about strengthening your family through delicious, beautiful meals worthy of Facebook posts, Pinterest, or even your own Food Network show. Maybe your imagination is already swirling with visions of perfectly set tables of fine china with all the kids in their best clothes dabbing at the corners of their mouths with dainty napkins as in *Downton Abbey*.

While your enthusiasm is definitely a tool to keep around, I'd caution you to remember the virtue of humility. Use "K.I.S.S.," or Keep It Simple (and) Sincere. Family meals don't have to be pretty—disposable dishes are fine! While home cooking is best, go ahead and get a store-bought roasted chicken when you need to. As long as you eat together and with the right intention, you'll be doing just great, in my opinion.

Acceptance is another great tool to have in your tool belt. You know you can't make an omelet without breaking a few eggs and you can't have nightly family meals without a few setbacks. It's best to make peace with it up front and be ready to go wherever this journey takes you.

If you are unsure of how you'll be able to make family mealtime work that is okay too. Simply have the willingness to fake it till you make it. Be willing to try again. Willing to learn. Willing to ask your kids what they think and then to incorporate their feedback.

Before moving on to step 5, take a moment to check that you have these three important tools in your toolbelt: humility, acceptance, and willingness.

❓ **DID YOU KNOW?** Pinterest stress is real! In a *Today* survey of seven thousand U.S. mothers, 42 percent said they suffer from Pinterest stress—i.e., the feeling that what they are doing is not worthy of posting online.[17] One mom even had to stop pinning altogether when a fun craft with her children ended in tears for everyone.

---

[17] Rebecca Dube, "'Pinterest Stress' Afflicts Nearly Half of Moms, Survey Says," *Today*, October 14, 2016, http://www.today.com/parents/pinterest-stress-afflicts-nearly-half-moms-survey-says-1C9850275.

Step 5: Make a Meal Plan

Home cooking is the goal. It lets you use fresh ingredients to provide healthy meals for your family. It provides the opportunity to cook and create a meal together and also to clean up as a team. But the struggles of life can compete with even the most organized cook. And hectic work schedules can interfere with even our best intentions.

What I'm trying to say is: don't feel guilty if you must occasionally lean on fast-food options or local restaurants to maintain a regular meal. Make your goal family togetherness not Martha Stewartness. Use your acceptance of the reality of your time constraints and your humility to provide what is achievable.

Even if the food is not home cooked, you can still make it home styled. In other words, you can maintain the same rituals, with everyone helping to set the table and clean up afterward. Always try to put the food on plates—even if it's carry-out. Serve each other. Give thanks. This may require you to call on that willingness in your toolbelt, but the extra effort can turn even "fast food" into a quality time for your family meal.

FAMILY STORY

The Horrible Cook

At the funeral of a beloved mother, the oldest child, with tears in his eyes, talked about what an awful cook she was. But he wasn't crying because of the food. He said that the fact that she tried so hard every day was the reason the family stayed together. By her actions, she showed them how important family was.

Step 6: The Family in Formation

The smell of delicious food can be a strong-enough magnet to pull together a busy family that is running in all directions! If your culinary skills aren't quite up to making good smells waft, however, or your children can't seem to get behind the idea of family meals, try expressing how important mealtime is to you.

When I was a child, I didn't like waiting to have dinner until my father got home. My mother explained how important it was to her. I didn't want to hurt her, so even if I pouted, I obeyed. Now that I'm older, I realize that waiting for the family meal told me that the people around the table were as important as the food on the table.

Reinforcing how happy you are to share the experience of eating together with your family will work better than exerting your will through force or discipline. Let them know that they are important to you and that this routine of family meals is an opportunity to grow and strengthen important relationships.

Home-Style Meal Options

Here are some back-pocket food options or strategies you can employ to help you keep your schedule:

- Food prepared in advance
- Come together to overcome difficulties
- Frozen leftovers (don't forget to thaw them properly)
- Pizza

- Supermarket café
- Frozen dinners
- Rotisserie chicken
- Take-out
- Fast food served with a side of something fresh

Write down the reason family mealtime is important, and tell it to your family:

_____

_____

_____

_____

_____

Pre-Dinner Snackage

If your schedules require you to have a late dinner, provide a small healthy snack to tide your kids over. They still have to practice waiting for the real meal, but they don't have to battle stomach rumblings while they do it. Remember these healthy-snack tips:

- water-based fruits and vegetables
- no false sugars
- small plates

Step 7: Consider the Conversation

Family mealtime gives us the opportunity to communicate with the people we love. The simple act of making regular family meals a priority tells our family members that we love them enough to commit to spending this time with them. It tells them that we care that they are fed and that we want to nurture them. Talking with one another, encouraging each child to share about his life, tells them they matter to us as individuals.

Admittedly, getting a teenager to share what happened that day can be like pulling teeth. It takes practice, and yes, there will be many frustrating moments. We'll explore specific tactics for different age groups later, but my fundamental approach to creating dinner discussions is the same no matter the age group. And I've seen it work in families all over the world.

Here's my secret: instead of trying to force your kids to talk, create an environment that fosters, encourages, and expects conversation. Consider it the F.E.E. to eat: Foster, Encourage, and Expect. Show kids what a healthy discussion looks like by engaging in one with your meal buddy, your spouse, or a dinner guest. Let lighter conversations open doors to explore topics and themes that are important to you as a family. Be ready to do some talking yourself, but also be willing to practice those listening skills.

> **❷ DID YOU KNOW?** Talking brings you closer. The word *converse* comes from the Latin *conversare*, "to turn constantly to." In sharing your experiences, hopes, and fears with each other, you are tearing down those subconscious mental walls that keep you apart. This ultimately helps your family members to turn to each other in times of need, working together as a family to overcome your obstacles and emerge on the other side stronger than ever.

Write at least five things that you want to communicate to your family by having regular meals:

_____

_____

_____

_____

_____

Step 8: Designate House "Specials"

Family meals let us be ourselves with each other. We relax into each other's presence at the end of a long day in shorts and flip-flops, and it's perfectly fine. These "familiar" meals help us form into a cohesive and intimate family.

Occasional formal meals, however, help to remind us not to take each other for granted. These could be on birthdays or holidays or to celebrate milestone moments. Whatever the cause, formal meals are great opportunities to give the family dinner extra-special attention. Get dressed up and take out the fancy plates. Your family is worth the fine china!

During these special dinners, we put on our best table manners and demonstrate the dignity of dining (rather than just eating). Without the experience of balancing formal and informal meals, we may grow up with little practice at formal table manners or, in the opposite direction, without the ability to be more casual and laid back during a meal.

List at least three special meals you want to share with your family this year:

Date: _____

Meal: _____

Date: _____

Meal: _____

Date: _____

Meal: _____

Step 9: Do It!

At the beginning of this chapter, I said that the only way to have family meals is just to do it. Now, at the end of this chapter, the same thing is still true.

But before you get all mad at me for making you read this chapter and do all the exercises, think about all the support and insight you've gained! You have:

- selected a meal buddy for support and accountability
- picked a time or set a schedule for family meals
- chosen ritual elements to include
- turned off your TV and put away your devices
- established reasonable expectations

- formulated backup plans to help you keep on schedule
- introduced the idea of regular meals to your family
- considered important topics you want to discuss during meals
- earmarked important dates you want to celebrate

So, although this step, "just do it," could easily have been step 1, I hope that going through these exercises has made you feel a lot less apprehension and fear. That tall high dive seems more like a step off the ledge into the kiddie pool now, right? You are ready, and I'm excited for you!

But one family meal does not a regular family meal make. This process will require ongoing effort and adjustments over time. Your supper-hero journey isn't over. That's why the following chapters explore how you can evolve and adapt family mealtime for different ages. For now, relax, knowing that you have mastered the fundamental approaches applied over the years and around the world to establish and strengthen the family through regular family meals.

EXERCISES

1. Good habits start here.

    Family mealtime is a great opportunity to practice good habits. Review some of the ways you can teach your children these important skills during family mealtime. Then pick one and incorporate it into your family mealtime ritual.

    - *Cooperation*: At family mealtime, everyone comes together as a family in pursuit of a common goal. How can you involve your other family members? Someone might help with preparing the food or putting it on plates or taking it to the table. Think of one way to involve each member of your family.
    - *Service*: Serving one another teaches selflessness. The more you are called on to serve, the less you feel entitled to be served. Think of one service that each family member could do for the others during family meals.
    - *Patience*: Waiting lets us practice patience. Look for opportunities to let your children practice this important skill. Maybe they need to wait for the water to boil or wait until everyone is finished eating to leave the table. Try giving your children the opportunity to practice patience over dinner tonight.

- *Problem solving*: Not everything is an argument that needs to be won immediately. When a conflict arises at the dinner table, try examining the problem instead of driving immediately to a solution. Let your children "chew" and "properly digest" the next problem that comes up. This will give you more chances for good conversation at tomorrow's dinner.
- *Gratitude*: This is another critical skill we all need to practice and there are many, many opportunities over dinner. Maybe it's being thankful for the food or recognizing that there are people who go without. Tonight, have each person say out loud something he is thankful for.

2. Just get started.

You might be circling around how to get started with family meals, like that age-old question about the chicken and the egg, but the most important thing is just to get started. So let's just use that egg and make dinner! Make it easy with three egg recipes beginning on page 114.

OPERATION FEEDING KIDS

Strategies for Meals with Young Children

Oh, the paradox of young children.[18] They rely on us for absolutely everything, but they still have complete dominion over our sleep schedules. And although it can be easier to make younger kids follow the rules, there's no guarantee that your infant won't reject a regular feeding schedule or your toddler won't refuse wholeheartedly to eat anything even remotely resembling green.

And with the simple act of providing nutrition proving difficult, you may be wondering how you can possibly feed your children all the other important things you know they need. Well, I'm happy to tell you that through pastoral counseling many, many families over the years, I've come across some proven strategies that make providing good nutrition, discipline, communication, and gratitude possible—from the very beginning.

---

[18] Even if you don't have young kids, don't skip ahead just yet.

The Milk Stage

New parents! Welcome to the club! I am not a cardholding member, but I have worked with enough young families to sympathize with them over the late nights, the fried brain cells, and the overwhelming desire to photograph every amazingly remarkable moment. In light of the whole fried-brain-cells thing, we'll keep this short and sweet.

- *Nutrition*: Feeding a newborn is more an art form than a science. It requires trial and error and, more importantly, keen observation. Your baby isn't going to ask for milk with some eloquent turn of phrase. It's up to you to respond to whatever your baby is putting out there—crying, screaming, staring at the ceiling fan. Yes, the most basic form of nutrition requires the most basic human trait—instinct. Trust that, and the rest will come.

- *Discipline*: Newborn minds develop at an amazing rate, and they are able to grasp new concepts all the time. When only several months old, a child begins to do things that aren't directly tied to the basic functions of eating, sleeping, and pooping—things such as grabbing jewelry or spitting food in your face. This is where discipline begins.[19] The word *discipline* is often misunderstood as punishment. It actually comes from the Latin *discipulus*, which means "pupil," and therefore concerns teaching! There are many ways to let your baby know that his behavior isn't appropriate. Parenting groups and books have lots of tips to get you started. Fair warning: this process often requires a whole lot more discipline on your part.

- *Communication*: This is not the life stage when we impart eternal words of wisdom, but we can still communicate very important messages to children. Gentleness and attention speak volumes. This is why we naturally employ "baby talk" when speaking to children. It's our instinctual way of laying the foundation for future healthy communication. Pay attention to what you are communicating to your infant.

❷ **DID YOU KNOW?** Baby talk is a conversation. Researchers at the University of Washington and the University of Connecticut recently confirmed that talking baby talk to infants helps them to master more words. What is also interesting is that one-on-one interactions that encourage the baby to "babble" back increase language advancement even more![20]

---

[19] See Jane Nelsen, Cheryl Erwin, and Roslyn Duffy, *Positive Discipline: The First Three Years*, rev. ed. (New York: Harmony Books, 2015).

[20] Molly McElroy, "Babbling Babies—Responding to One-on-One 'Baby Talk'—Master More Words," *UW News*, January 6, 2014, http://www.washington.edu/news/2014/01/06/babbling-babies-responding-to-one-on-one-baby-talk-master-more-words/.

From Purée to People Food

As infants grow, you add to their diet, which serves as the perfect analogy for how you should also be adding to how you discipline, nurture, and teach them. It's a slow, gradual transition that requires that everything be kept soft and easily digestible.

- *Nutrition*: Infants transition from milk to puréed foods and, eventually, to morsels from our plates. The food is always simple and soft. They need it to be easily digestible, but their physiology is also changing, allowing them to eat more and more "grown-up" food all the time. Again, pay attention to what they can handle while ensuring that they get the nutrition they need.

- *Discipline*: Discipline is a process. A good place to start is "food doesn't come when you cry." You can also establish the dinner table as something different from other places where your child might eat, with certain expectations. All the while, remember to keep any discipline soft—just like those puréed foods. Your infant is learning all the time, but as with newborns (and spoiler alert: *any* age), discipline at this stage requires a lot of discipline on your part. Don't lose hope! Don't lose your cool. They *will* learn you aren't supposed to throw Cheerios on the ground. Just maybe not today.

- *Communication*: When we raise our voices with the bitterness of anger or the spiciness of rage, we are force-feeding children something they can't digest well. Do your best to maintain a softer, sweeter, more "puréed" home environment and speaking tone. Also pay close attention to what your children need from you. This will be different for each child and will shift as they age. But it's important to remember that we hunger for spiritual, emotional, and intellectual nourishment, not just physical.

- *Gratitude*: I can't stress enough how important gratitude is. I encounter children, teenagers, and adults who feel completely entitled; and they all possess very little gratitude. Even those of us with hardships have things to be grateful for and can take comfort in this. Do your best to make gratitude a natural part of the menu, even if it's just you saying "please" and "thank you."

FAMILY STORY

Mealtime Is a Gift

I hate to see kids sent away from the dinner table, but I understand that different things work for different children. One technique I loved was when a father took his son away from the table to have a talk about his behavior. I was a guest, and the son really wanted my attention, so he was acting up. After his talk with his father, the boy let his parents "have a turn" talking with Father Leo too.

❷ DID YOU KNOW? You can help your child to learn to read from the table. Dinnertime conversation boosts vocabulary acquisition in young children even more than being read to aloud![21] Introducing new words also helps your children to learn to read earlier and more easily.

Bite-Size Meals

Here we go, folks: the terrible twos and beyond! From the moment they are eating bite-size food until you pack them up for their first day of preschool, children are constantly expanding their diet and their world. Increasing complexity is the name of the game now, and the key is to keep it all bite-size.

- *Nutrition*: Guide your children as they explore and investigate new foods. Expand their horizons, and do your best to keep them from getting stuck on eating only certain foods. Introduce the importance of eating things that are good for you, but just like their methodically cut-up meals, keep all of the concepts you talk about bite-size. And if they just won't eat it today, don't despair. You may learn a new recipe! Baked kale chips are now a cool color "potato" chip in some households!

- *Discipline*: Make sure your children know what is expected at the dinner table. As they learn the rules, hold them to proper table manners. Make dinner an opportunity to practice "please" and "thank you" and sharing. You can also start to build some "bite-size" rituals, such as helping to set the table by first putting the napkins out or helping to clear the table by taking their plates to the sink. As you increase what you ask of your children, remember to instill discipline as an opportunity for them to demonstrate their love for their family. Helping

FAMILY STORY

They Wanted to Try What They Made

A couple I met developed a wonderful strategy when their kids began refusing to try new foods, specifically vegetables. Instead of just trying new ways to cook the food, they had their kids help them in the kitchen. They might wash vegetables or stir a pot of soup. In the end, their kids were more interested in trying the food they helped to make. And they started eating more new foods!

---

[21] Anne K. Fishel, "It's Science: Eat Dinner Together," The Family Dinner Project, posted by Bri DeRosa, January 27, 2015, http://thefamilydinnerproject.org/food-for-thought/science-eat-dinner-together/.

Mom or Dad is never a punishment and should not be presented as such.

- *Communication*: Kids will keep asking why from now until eternity. It's up to you to make sure that your answers to even their most gargantuan questions are "bite-size." Feel free to talk about important topics and give them plenty to "chew" on. But practice portion control, lest these healthy lessons—much like that extra portion of healthy broccoli—go to waste.

- *Gratitude:* Satisfy some of this age group's notorious inquisitiveness by letting them see where food comes from. This could involve a trip to a farm or a farmer's market, growing a garden, or planting herbs. As they begin to understand that their meals don't materialize out of thin air, their gratitude for the food they eat will grow along with the seeds you plant.

FAMILY STORY

You Know Your Children Best

Researchers at the Yale Parenting Center have noted many creative solutions that parents have found that work for their kids, but that no technique works for every child.*

A family I know developed an amazing way to end arguments between their grade-school children: they announced a game of tag. The quarrel evaporated in the opportunity to enjoy each other's company instead.

* Andrea Peterson, "Smarter Ways to Discipline Children," *Wall Street Journal*, December 24, 2012, http://www.wsj.com/articles/SB10001424127887323277504578189680045268049.

---

❷ DID YOU KNOW? Goldfish have longer attention spans than people do. Microsoft conducted a study on the impact of smartphones on human attention spans.[22] Since 2000, our attention spans have decreased by about 4 seconds, putting us one second below goldfish. On a positive note, the same study showed that our ability to multitask has improved.

---

[22] Leon Watson, "Humans Have Shorter Attention Span Than Goldfish, Thanks to Smartphones," *Telegraph*, May 15, 2015, http://www.telegraph.co.uk/science/2016/03/12/humans-have-shorter-attention-span-than-goldfish-thanks-to-smart/.

Did Suzie Get Her Veggies Too?

Many parents I talk to struggle to get their children to eat vegetables. One dad shared a unique strategy! His daughter loved her doll Suzie. She took her everywhere, but Suzie wasn't allowed at the dinner table. One night, the dad had an idea. Why doesn't Suzie come to dinner? He put out a chair and set a place, and during the meal, he asked his daughter if Suzie should eat her vegetables. Wanting to be a good mom, the girl said yes, she should, because they are good for her. The dad suggested that his daughter show Suzie how to eat vegetables, and she did. She was happy to set a good example for her doll!

Keepin' It Appetizing

When children enter kindergarten or first grade, they continue to investigate and begin asserting their likes and dislikes more and more often. Sometimes those dislikes are things that we know are good for them. Here's how you can make sure that nutrition, discipline, communication, and gratitude stay appetizing as your children grow into their unique selves throughout grade school.

- *Nutrition*: Getting children to eat vegetables comes down to making the vegetables as desirable as possible. Step 1: tell your child how important it is to eat healthy food. Step 2: make the food tasty. You aren't doing yourself any favors by boiling Brussels sprouts, believe me. Sauté them with a little bacon! And look for more ways to make nutritious foods indulgently delicious—think roasted veggies, goat cheese, and herbs! If you put your best foot forward, and your children still don't like the dish, try having them describe why they don't like it, and see if you can make it better. If nothing works, go back to step 1 and be ready to employ a little discipline.

- *Discipline*: It is time to make the full transition from "I eat when I cry" to: "I wait to eat until we are all together because family togetherness is important"; "I eat what my parents provide because they are trying to give me a healthy future"; "I help with our family meal because we all need to love and serve each other." This might seem like a large pill to get your kid to swallow, but you can make it appetizing in the same way you made Brussels sprouts appetizing. It's all in the preparation. Prepare your children for these disciplines by increasing what they contribute to the meal, each time coating it with desirable things such as family, well-being, and love.

- *Communication*: Young children are like sponges, and dinnertime is your opportunity to give them something good to absorb. The key at this stage is not to force-feed them.

Model the good behavior you want them to have. Eat the good foods you want them to eat. And let them soak it up. Now is also a good time to begin the practice of dinner conversations. Like adding new flavors to the menu, bringing up things you think they might find interesting will keep dinnertime appetizing.

• *Gratitude*: The simple act of participating in the family meal does more than provide discipline; it reinforces your children's appreciation for the time and energy that go into creating dinner. Provide additional opportunities to help them make this connection. Take them fishing, or give them the responsibility to water the herb garden. Have them see that food isn't just picked; it's grown. Each meal takes time, love, and care. Get your children to articulate their appreciation for this during each meal, and you'll be giving them a daily opportunity to practice gratitude.

You may be thinking this is all just too much to think about, considering that you're struggling with the mechanics of just getting everyone around the dinner table every night. Not to

Kid Contributions

There are many ways your children can participate in mealtime. Start small, but always look for increasing responsibilities as they age. Here are some tips parents have shared with me over the years. It will take patience on your part to handle spills or mistakes, but let your children learn, and reward their contributions with your gratitude.

Before the Meal
• set the table
• wash vegetables
• measure and mix ingredients
• take food to the table

During the Meal
• employ table manners
• pass the food to others before serving themselves
• say "thank you" for the food

After the Meal
• clear the table
• rinse the dishes
• help load the dishwasher
• wipe down the countertops
• put food away
• package any leftovers

worry. You don't have to address everything all at once! Do what you can tonight, and try to add something else tomorrow. That's the beauty of regular meals. There's always the next one!

You might also be thinking that this would all be much easier with only one kid! That's true, but only to a degree. Whether you have one kid or one dozen, you can still teach nutrition, discipline, communication, and gratitude during the family meal. In fact, in larger families, the older children can make family meals easier. Older siblings can model good behavior or take over small tasks. Think of it as simply more ways you can involve kids with the meal. I've witnessed many older siblings learning more about nutrition, discipline, communication, and gratitude by teaching it to their younger siblings. I've also witnessed older teenagers become angst-filled problem causers, but we'll deal with that in a later chapter.

The bottom line is you have to find what works for you. Take it one stage at a time, and everything will go fine. It won't go perfectly, but then again, what do we expect from imperfect people we call "family" — of which you and I are imperfect parts?

EXERCISES

1. Get up to speed.

    If you aren't starting at the milk stage, it is absolutely okay. The important thing, after all, is to get family meals cooking *now*, whenever now is. Review all the stages in this chapter, and assess where your kids are with nutrition, discipline, communication, and gratitude. Then identify some activities you can do with your children to strengthen them in the areas where they could use some help. Even if your children are already in grade school, dinner is still the perfect opportunity to practice saying "please" and "thank you" with sincerity. And if your older children aren't used to contributing to the family, start "bite-size" and build, one meal at a time. Don't rush or force-feed. Work to ease them from foundational things such as clearing their plates to more-involved meal participation.

2. Discipline means you too.

    Sometimes teaching discipline requires more discipline from us. You need to be ready to stick with your rules and consistently apply them. This can be taxing and draining, but being disciplined yourself can help your children learn more quickly. What are some things you can do to stick to your dinner rituals and other family meal goals?

3. Put away technology.

Let's face it: we are all a little addicted to our smartphones. Talk to your spouse or your meal buddy for support and to stay accountable for putting technology away during dinner. Also, use your support to keep you honest about where your attention is. Make sure out of sight is out of mind, and you are not drafting e-mail or text responses in your head during dinner. Being focused and engaged on the family discussions happening around you can make all the difference.

4. Let your family enjoy the same food in different ways.

Even if everyone in your family can't eat the same dish, they can eat the same food. See the simple to the sophisticated and tasty recipes on page 118.

MISSION IMPOSSIBLE

Strategies for Meals with Teenagers

Parents are often bewildered to discover that their little vegetable-eating angels have been replaced by eye-rolling teenagers seemingly overnight. No matter what they do, their teens still retreat behind smartphone screens, soundproof ear buds, and closed bedroom doors. This new distance is often part of the process of growing up, and I believe it's also a major reason why regular family meals drop by nearly 20 percent as children become teenagers.[23]

> ❷ **DID YOU KNOW?** Eating regular meals improves teen performance. Teens who regularly eat with their parents are: 1.5 times less likely to report high levels of stress; 2 times as likely to get As in school; and 1.5 times more likely to have strong relationships with their parents.

---

23 M. W. Gillman et al., "Family Dinner and Diet Quality among Older Children and Adolescents," *Archives of Family Medicine* 9, no. 3 (March 2000), posted at National Center for Biotechnology Information, https://www. ncbi.nlm.nih.gov/pubmed/10728109.

That's not to say that teens are "ruining" family meals on purpose. They are going through a lot of changes—not only biologically and psychologically but socially, emotionally, and just about every other "-ally" you can think of. Everything about their world is shifting and changing as they grow and learn new things about the world and themselves.

This is also a difficult time for you! Instead of being completely responsible for your hormone-crazed children, you are starting to shift more and more responsibility into their not-entirely-ready-to-handle-it hands. You're balancing disciplining them with respecting their independence, protecting them with lending them the keys to a motor vehicle, and more—all while changing the way you parent to match your teenagers' new level of arguable maturity.

In the midst of all these changes and challenges, mealtime can be that point on the horizon that guides your child safely through the storm of teenagerdom. I know it is much easier said than done, but all you need to do is keep having regular meals together.

> ❷ **DID YOU KNOW?** Teens enjoy eating with their families. Research shows that a majority of teens desire having meals with their families. In fact, a study showed that over 90 percent of teens enjoy family mealtimes. And one survey showed that spending time with their family is what makes them happiest.[24] And we all know that good food makes everyone happy!

What to Feed Teens

Teens typically choose what they eat for two of the three meals they eat each day, which means it's more important than ever to reinforce healthy habits. As with other areas of their lives, help your teens to find the information they need to make the right food choices for themselves.

For example, if your teens are big on sports, stress the importance of protein to build muscles. If they want to lose weight (and it is healthy for them to do so), teach them about empty calories. Discuss how food fuels the body and explore how taking time to give your body the right food can be better than reaching for the fast-food solution.

This is probably the last time you will have any sort of influence over what your children eat. Once they move out on their own, they are going to eat what they want, when they want. Try to give them the right framework so they will be ready when the time comes. At the same time,

---

[24] SWNS, "Teenagers Spend Nearly 1,000 Hours Obsessing about Food," *New York Post*, May 30, 2018, https://nypost.com/2018/05/30/teenagers-spend-nearly-1000-hours-obsessing-about-food/; Associated Press and MTV, *Youth Happiness Study* (New York: Associated Press, 2007), 2, http://surveys.ap.org/data/Knowledge-Networks/2007-08-20%20AP-MTV%20Youth%20Happiness.pdf.

your teens need to be "fed" a lot more than nutrition science, because your teens are no doubt craving something else in addition to junk food.

Give Them What They Want

Every teenager wants to be treated like a respected adult, right? You remember that from your own experience. Adults are "free" to make their own decisions. But adults know that their decisions have repercussions—good and bad—and they are responsible for the consequences of their actions.

Do you see where I'm going with this?

Adults must be responsible, so the best way to help your children transition into adulthood is to give them responsibilities! There are many areas in which your teens can demonstrate their maturity by fulfilling their obligations. And just as the family meal was the perfect time for younger children to practice discipline, gratitude, communication, and other important life skills, it is the perfect time for teenagers to practice being responsible.

FAMILY STORY
Introducing Family Meals to Teens

One of the recipe testers from my first book never established regular family meals. He told me that he wanted to start but was afraid that his teenagers would make it difficult. I encouraged him to share with his children what he had shared with me: that he thought family meals together would make the family stronger in a good, fun, healthy way. Later, he told me that his children surprised him by how they rallied around family meals once they understood why he wanted to have them.

Decide what responsibilities make sense for your teens. Then help them to see that fulfilling those responsibilities is what it feels like to be treated as an adult. Explain that this is what contributing to the family looks like for a mature, responsible person. Help them to understand that in giving them these obligations, you are really doing what *they* want. You are starting to treat them as adults.

> ❷ DID YOU KNOW? Despite how they want to be treated, teens don't feel like adults. According to a 2016 survey, only 27 percent of Americans feel like adults at eighteen. The definition seems to be less about age and more about financial dependence.[25]

---

[25] Bank of America and *USA Today*, *Better Money Habits Report: Young Americans and Money* (Fall 2016): 3.

Ways to Treat Your Teens Like Adults

Here are a few ways to provide experiences of maturity before, during, and after mealtime:

- Ask your teens to help create the family menu for the week.
- Put them in charge of the shopping list.
- Get them to take over the grocery runs (especially if they're practicing their driving skills).
- Invite them to take part in cooking the meal.

- Challenge them to display good table manners.
- Ask them to recommend a farmers' market or local farm to visit as a family.
- Get them to find a soup kitchen or another organization where the family can volunteer.
- Put them in charge of making a dish for special occasions.

The New "Time Out"

Since you are starting to treat your children as adults, the dynamic of "discipline" needs to change. You wouldn't put an adult in time out, for example. But you can't simply stop disciplining your children. Remember, *discipline* means teaching, not punishing, and although teenagers think they know everything, they still have a lot to learn.

Different things work for different teens, but one idea I've seen be very successful at the dinner table is what one couple called their "incentive" program. They explained it like an incentive program at work. Their teen earned the privilege of being treated like an adult by doing the daily mealtime chores. If the teen failed to hold up his end of the bargain, he would be reprimanded like an employee who showed up late for work.

The objective is not simply to entice your kids to do their mealtime chores as you might have bribed them to try broccoli by promising dessert. Rather, you are using the reward of responsibility as a means of helping your children to mature.

As you think about the right "incentive program" for your teens, be sure to use what you learned about your children's temperaments in chapter 2. That will help to ensure that the program is a good fit to discipline your children.

Talking "Teenager"

Many supper heroes have trouble with dinner-time conversation as their children transition into teenagers. Talking to teens can be like learning (or relearning) a language. I've found that teens' shorter attention spans require fewer words and more meaning. In other words, the "what" you are communicating has to be clear and to the point.

I also use my "boring filter" during conversations. To me, boring is when someone answers a question that no one is asking. If the teens aren't interested in the topic, I think of ways to make it interesting. Or I save it for a later date. I also listen for the question they want to ask but haven't asked. That's the information they want to hear.

Of course, they'll hear what I'm saying only if I use the right tone. Teens aren't children anymore, so in addition to what you are communicating to them, you must pay attention to *how* you are communicating. Sounding overly authoritative or "preachy" (even I avoid this tone) can seem patronizing. And raising your voice in anger or frustration isn't helpful at all. It just feeds into the vortex of spiraling emotions in their already overly dramatic lives.

FAMILY STORY
Earning Screen Time

Many families struggle with the proper use of Internet-connected devices. One family shared a smart way they used screen time as their teen's new "time out." This teen had a job and could theoretically pay for his phone and monthly phone bill. The parents, however, let their teen "pay" his monthly bill with good behavior. Bad behavior meant that he didn't earn his phone that month. He had to pay up or forfeit the phone.

These parents took the "lose the favorite toy" concept from when their child was little and updated it to involve financial repercussions. This acted as a new time out and also taught their teen about financial responsibilities and the realities of owning and using a phone.

❷ **DID YOU KNOW?** Teens' inattention is biological. Teenagers' brains are still developing; this causes more activity in the prefrontal cortex and affects teenagers' ability to multitask.[26] I've found that when I keep my dialogue with teens in its most "tweetable" form (140 characters or less), I keep their attention longer.

---

[26] Iroise Dumontheil, Bano Hassan, Sam J. Gilbert and Sarah-Jayne Blakemore, "Development of the Selection and Manipulation of Self-Generated Thoughts in Adolescence," *Journal of Neuroscience* 30, no. 2 (June 2, 2010), https://doi.org/10.1523/JNEUROSCI.1375-10.2010; "Why Teenagers Can't Concentrate," *Dawn*, June 1, 2010, https://www.dawn.com/news/814160/why-teenagers-can-t-concentrate.

The Drama-Free Zone

Solving problems and resolving issues undoubtedly becomes increasingly important during the turbulent teen years. But it's still important to keep these solution-driven discussions from the dinner table as much as possible. I'm not saying you should ignore or bury issues just because you want a "pleasant" meal. You need to discuss these things, certainly, but try not to ruin the encouraging-dinner-discussion environment you've been cultivating by giving your teens a double serving of difficult topics.

Instead, let dinner be the "ice breaker" for solving problems together later. Bring up issues, or let your children bring them up, but relegate solutions to another time and place. For example, instead of "What are you going to do about that D in math class?" try "Let's go over that math test after dinner."

As your children grow, you will also find yourself needing a time and place to discuss things like romantic relationships, drugs and alcohol, rule breaking, and so forth. I've found that many families find success when they set up regular times, weekly or monthly, where they can have one-on-one time with each child. These special bonding activities provide the perfect opportunity for the deeper discussions you want to keep away from the dinner table.

When—Not If—the Shiitake Hits the Fan

Blowups, scream fests, and all-out emotional breakdowns can happen, do happen, and will happen. I can't even try to tell you how to resolve these, because each fight requires its own solution. And it's up to each family to find the solution that works best for them.

Although no one likes an argument, there are some very powerful lessons that can be learned from them. Working through problems and tensions helps children learn conflict resolution and other key skills they'll need in their adult lives. These experiences also give the whole family important lessons in forgiveness.

The blessing of regular meals is that everyone will come back together again at the next scheduled time. Life will move on. The family will stay together, stronger for having overcome the difficulty as a team.

Teens and Lack of Respect

"This all sounds nice, *but my teen doesn't respect me!*" This is the most common reason why families I work with say they want to abandon the family meal. But please, if your teens won't respect your wishes and participate, don't be defeated. Don't let their disrespect be the reason you give up.

In working with many families, I've discovered that disrespect is *never* the problem. It's merely a symptom of the problem. You can use the pressure cooker steps above to engage with your teens and root out the underlying cause of their bad attitude.

But before you try opening up the heated pressure cooker, it may be helpful to cool things down in your own head and heart. Quit self-defeating or dramatic urges and give yourself the space calmly to examine why your teens may be disrespecting you.

The Pressure Cooker Method, a.k.a. Handling Resistance

If you've ever worked with a pressure cooker, you know the three simple steps necessary to "tenderize" teenagers who are hard-set against regular family meals:

1. Put on the lid correctly: *put family meals on the nonnegotiable list.*
2. Pay attention to how long the pot is heating up: *pay attention to how your child may be "heating up" during the discussion.*
3. Take off the lid *only after* the pot is cool: *let things cool down before trying to open up dialogue again.*

Your teens know that you have a great personal investment in family togetherness and are having regular meals to strengthen the family. If they're still resistant after going through the method outlined above a couple of times, don't give in or give up.

I have seen families enter into the regular-family-meals game late and get unruly teenagers to sit down civilly every night! It is possible. Just be like the pressure cooker. Don't apply too much heat, and don't forget to let things cool down before trying again to open up your teens' hearts and minds. With time and consistency, you can tenderize even the hardest-hearted teenager.

FAMILY STORY

Even Supper Heroes Need Practice

I always go back to humility because it is easy to get caught up in the idea that Father or Mother "knows best," which is often perpetuated by our society. This was the case for me recently.

One day, I got really upset with my mother because she gave instructions to someone that completely contradicted mine. My dad got pretty angry with me, saying that I needed to be more respectful. I reflected on the situation and realized that my getting upset was not rooted in disrespect—it was rooted in my being angry that my mother disregarded my opinion.

By ignoring what I wanted, my mother was showing *me* disrespect. Yes, it can happen that supper heroes are disrespectful to their children. After I calmly and respectfully explained this to my parents, they realized that I *do* respect them. From that experience, I learned that my parents and I respect each other, and we do so enough to discuss why we get upset.

Ask yourself:

- Am I pushing too hard, or forcing them to be like other "perfect" families?
- Do I respect their uniqueness by asking *them* the best way to communicate with them about important matters, such as family dinners?
- Are my teenagers in the right place to hear what I'm saying?
- Where did they learn how to become such "brats," and have I talked calmly with them about better behavior?
- I keep asking for their respect, but did I earn it? Do I respect them?

Remember, respect is a two-way street. It's extremely difficult to respect someone who doesn't respect you. If the reflection above doesn't give you enough insight into why your teens may be acting the way they are, see exercise 5 at the end of this chapter for more ideas on this topic.

Including Friends

At this age, friends can almost become more important than family. Don't fight this. Positive friendships can be a huge support for your teens as they navigate the rocky waters of adolescence.

If your kids' best friends dress in black and have a few piercings, a chip on their shoulder, or a penchant for letting people know they're zealous vegans—go ahead and make room for them at your table. This sense of "welcoming others" shows your teens that a healthy family includes—not excludes. Family dinners also give you the opportunity to help your teens strengthen healthy friendships.

I remember when my siblings' friends would come over for dinner. It was weird to see another person at the table, but it was even more interesting to see these "guests" (my siblings' friends) help set the table and clean up afterward. My parents were happy not only to serve the friends as guests but also to see them as part of the family.

> ❷ **DID YOU KNOW?** Trusted friendships decrease risky behavior. According to a 2015 study by Dr. Eva Telzer of the University of Illinois, teens with friends they trust are less likely to engage in risky behaviors such as riding with a dangerous driver or shoplifting.[27]

Global Family

Including people who are important to your children in the mechanics of family life helps foster a deeper, more wholesome and realistic understanding of family. So does providing opportunities to give back to our global family, the human race.

Many young people are filled with optimistic enthusiasm for being a part of something greater. Help them harness this energy with opportunities to give back to the local and global community. On the other hand, many young people also have a self-centered mentality, which keeps them focused on activities that serve or benefit them. Either way, helping your teens to develop an appreciation for giving back is vital to their transformation into responsible adults.

I've seen the positive effects of serving others countless times. Kids who serve others are more likely to develop the virtue of humility and gratitude—necessary characteristics of an independent person. They almost always have a deeper understanding of their responsibility to people, places, and things beyond themselves.

As your teenagers continue to grow and mature, take advantage of any opportunity you have to show them how a true adult helps another person in need.

> ❷ **DID YOU KNOW?** Volunteering benefits are scientifically proven! We all know that helping others makes us feel good, but researchers at the London School of Economics were able to chart the connection between helping others and happiness. They found that people who volunteer build more empathy, have stronger social bonds, and even smile more![28]

---

[27] Sue Shellenbarger, "What Teens Need Most from Their Parents," *Wall Street Journal*, August 10, 2016, https://www.wsj.com/articles/what-teens-need-most-from-their-parents-1470765906.

[28] Mark Horoszowski, "5 Surprising Benefits of Volunteering," *Forbes*, March 19, 2015, https://www.forbes.com/sites/nextavenue/2015/03/19/5-surprising-benefits-of-volunteering/#5099ddb8127b.

EXERCISES

1. **Remember when you were a teen.**

   It's easy to look at teenagers as if they are aliens. Remembering that we were just as hormone-fueled and "know it all" when we were their age is humbling. But a humble family is a happy one. And reflecting on your youth is a great way to get in touch with who your teenagers are right now and what they're going through.

2. **Give your teens responsibility.**

   Review the list of responsibilities suggested in this chapter, and think about how else you can start treating your teens as adults. What will work for your children as individuals? What can they do that will contribute to your family in particular?

3. **Try the new "time out."**

   What adult responsibility are your children itching to earn? What things will motivate them to learn to fulfill their obligations to the family? Sketch out the "incentive program" that will best motivate your teen. Also be ready to take away those adult privileges when your teens don't live up to their end of the bargain.

4. **Set aside "one-on-one" time.**

   One-on-one time doesn't have to be an entire afternoon. Even a late-night cup of tea or a trip to the concession stand during an older sibling's soccer game can do the trick. These times will be important when issues that you want to talk about arise. So, be sure to have them in place before you need them.

5. **Remember that respect is a two-way street.**

   Whether you are in the right (or in the wrong), you can always respectfully approach someone important to you to get to the underlying reason for that person's disrespect. Asking a few questions with clear, direct, drama-free language will help you get to the root of the problem with your teens.

Try the following with your disrespecting teenager:

- What do we need to learn about each other to treat each other with respect?
- What was the reason for your getting upset and treating me so disrespectfully?
- Where did you learn such disrespectful behavior?
- How can I help you treat others more respectfully?
- If you continue with your disrespect, how can you expect me or others to respect you?

These questions may sound unrealistically "reasonable," but to communicate clearly how we are feeling we often need to let reason take the lead. In putting our emotions aside, we allow ourselves to focus on getting to the root of the problem. And by humbling ourselves to explore rationally how our actions might be upsetting someone else, we demonstrate the most important emotion of all: love.

6. Get your teens involved in the kitchen.

Let your teens help you make delicious chicken tenders and use the leftovers in a salad—with customizable homemade dressing—for lunch the next day. See the recipes on pages 121 and 122.

CHAPTER

7

EXPEDITION INDEPENDENCE TRAINING WHEELS

Strategies for Meals with Young Adults

You've heard the saying "Give a man some fish, and he eats for a day. Teach him to fish, and he eats for a lifetime." Well, it's the same with self-reliance. Sort of. The difference is that your children can't truly understand what it means to be self-reliant until they're no longer dependent on you. Which is why it's time for your little fishermen to start casting the line without you!

Whether your kids are going off to college or trade school or are starting a profession, they are taking big steps toward independence. This is an exciting time, and it is normal to have mixed emotions. Many parents I work with experience a bittersweet melancholy knowing that things will never be the same. My own parents get sentimental reflecting on the "good ol' days"—and we still share meals at least twice a month!

Although it's completely normal to feel a tugging at your heartstrings when your children leave the nest, it's important not to let these feelings keep you from sending your children off on their own. They need a gentle shove out of the nest to be able to fly. If you're having trouble, I recommend doing what many of the parents I work with do—what my own parents told me they did—keep your eyes on the prize.

> ❷ **DID YOU KNOW?** Parents are the main reason kids say they don't feel like adults. A majority of young Americans (62 percent) don't feel like adults until they are in their twenties. An overwhelming 80 percent say they don't feel like adults because they rely on their parents for support.[29] On the plus side, the main reason young Americans gave for feeling like adults was preparation from their parents.

You want your children to become independent. That's the goal—the prize—you've been working toward for nearly two decades. You are so close. Don't give up now. Continue giving them what they need to succeed—which, in this case, is the opportunity to experience complete independence from you.

That's not to say that your role as a supper hero is over. Far from it! Your children may be starting to depend on themselves, but they still have a lot to learn from you about independence. And they'll always need you to "share some fish" with them. This is why keeping regular meals intact during this transitional phase is critical. There's a lot of maturing and formation left to do after all, and the best place to do it is still around the dinner table.

> ❷ **DID YOU KNOW?** Financial independence is the number-one mark of adulthood. Thirty-nine percent of young adults ranked financial independence as the milestone that most defined adulthood. Others answered moving out on their own (14 percent), completing their education (7 percent), and getting married or starting a family (7 percent).[30]

Letting Go

I often joke that the only reason the prodigal son (Luke 15:11–32) wanted to come home was because he was hungry and needed to do his laundry! But in the story, the father loved his son

---

[29] Bank of America and *USA Today*, *Better Money Habits Report*, 3.
[30] Ibid.

enough to let him go and make his own mark in the world. Then, when the young man wanted to return home, his father welcomed him with open arms despite his mistakes.

The prodigal son learned important life lessons the hard way, and many children have similar growing pains. Protecting your children from these lessons will deny them opportunities to understand independence. Instead, be like the father in the story, and encourage your children to take the lead in their own lives.

Before-They-Go Checklist

In a recent study, young Americans reported wishing they knew more about cooking, laundry, household chores, and financial planning before leaving the home.* Here are some "easy to overlook" life lessons kids should know before leaving home:

- the difference between dishwasher detergent and dish soap—silly but true!
- that air fresheners work effectively only if you take out the trash and do your laundry
- cooking basics (how to use a Crock-Pot and a hot pad—and what *not* to microwave)
- how to manage monthly bills and other budgeting necessities

- the best way to pick out fresh versus ripening veggies
- how to make the most of leftovers and not to waste food
- healthy planning and brain-food snack recipes
- *and most importantly*: they can always come home for a family meal!

* Ibid., 5.

My parents used to joke that their job was done when I was able to: (1) make money and balance my checkbook, (2) pray on my own without their "forcing" me to go to church, and (3) cook a meal and share it with friends. Think about what your children need to be independent. Then, bit by bit, provide them with increasing responsibility so that eventually they don't need to depend on you for these things.

➤🍴 FOOD FOR THOUGHT

Financial Irresponsibility in the First Year of College Is a Warning Sign

The University of Arizona found that financial behaviors in late adolescence were strongly tied to financial behaviors in adulthood, particularly when it came to financial decisions made in the first year of college.* While sociodemographic characteristics didn't seem to influence the transition, the highly financially responsible students had better financial attitudes, higher parental expectations and financial education.

* University of Arizona, *Life After College: Drivers for Young Adult Success* (Tucson: University of Arizona, 2014), 8, 27, http://aplus.arizona.edu/wave-3-report.pdf.

Letting go of certain parental responsibilities, which have become habit over the years, may be difficult. It's nice to feel needed, and doing things for others is a way many of us show that we care. It can help to remember that you are still a part of your children's lives, even if you aren't providing these things anymore. The opportunity to experience true independence is the greatest gift you can give your young adults.

The Training Wheels Are Still On

While you are letting go and preparing your children to go it alone as adults, it's important to remember that they aren't quite there yet. At this stage in their lives, they still need a lot of formation. The analogy of training wheels has helped many of the parents I work with to understand their function at this stage.

You are your young adults' training wheels, guiding them along the way and letting them fail while never truly letting them fall. It's a hard balancing act. But you know your children best and are best equipped to determine the "training wheels approach" that will prepare them for adulthood.

The good news is that there is still a regular opportunity for you to see where your child may need some course correcting. This avenue also offers great opportunities to engage in discussions about important topics and offer formation. Of course, I am talking about the family meal!

Keeping the Family Meal Alive

Young adults lead, by necessity, a very fluid, transitional life. They're always on the go. That's why the regular meal is so important. It keeps young adults connected to the family and becomes a symbol of stability in the midst of their dramatically changing world. This is true even as the meal goes through a transition.

When your adult children achieve independence, regular meals as a family also have to change. You will not be able to eat together as regularly as you once did, and you as a parent will never again have as much uncontested authority. Your children are independent adults, free to make their own decisions. This means you need to stay vigilant to keep family meals from fading away.

I've seen it happen countless times. One dinner gets pushed because of a late-night study session, another because of a child's work schedule. Before you know it, the regularity of family meals is thrown to the wayside, and you're left with important holidays or birthdays and little else.

While things will never again be the same as when your children were young, make sure you all stay on the same page about how important family meals are. The dinner table is where your family can offer each other love and support. It's a place for family rituals and traditions. And it's where you can still provide opportunities for formation—even if your methods are more sophisticated than using a pretend airplane to feed your kids their veggies.

> **FAMILY STORY**
> ## I Didn't Want to Wait for a Holiday
> There are many "built-in" opportunities for regular family meals, such as religious or civic holidays, birthdays, and anniversaries. But one mother told me she didn't want to wait for a holiday to get together. Instead, her family turned the first Thursday of every month into a family holiday. They made their own holiday, and you can too!

Discuss the Transition as a Family

Many families I've worked with struggle to keep regular meals going through adulthood. One thing I've seen work for a lot of families is to have a serious talk before the children leave the nest.

You may have discussed the importance of family meals in the past, but this time you are having the conversation with your children as adults. Again, explain all the benefits the meal provides, and ask for their input. Then get your children to work with you to create a schedule that allows the family to continue having regular meals together. I've heard that this family meeting is very beneficial even for families with children who have already left home. There are often just more growing pains as the family reworks itself into a regular routine.

Easy Does It

Some parents feel that their young adults won't come home for a meal as often as they would like. Almost as many young adults feel pressured or obligated to come home more often than they want to. It's important that both sides communicate and respect each other's needs. The biggest thing is often for parents to remember that they are letting go.

Even if your children are just in the next town, or in the basement, for that matter, it's important to respect that they have other commitments. At the same time, don't feel as if you have to bend over backward to accommodate their schedules. Feel empowered to put the responsibility of scheduling family meals on your children. This is another opportunity for them to mature while demonstrating or experiencing fidelity to the family. The key is that regular family meals are set ahead of time and then kept.

With regular meals, your children know they still have a place to come when they need a little rest stop along the path to adulthood—especially if that path takes surprising turns.

Keep an Eye Out

Until their children leave the nest, many parents witness all of the changes they undergo gradually. So, when they come home after a few months away, it's easier to see what has changed. It

---

Formation at a Distance

Your young adults no longer need (or want) you to look over their shoulder. At the same time, young adults still need a fair amount of formation, and regular communication is a great way to provide this—especially if you are going months between meals.

Different things work for different families, but I've learned that scheduling weekly phone calls, video chats, or e-mails is very helpful through this transition. Even a text now and then provides supper heroes with an avenue for tapping into more regular formation outside of the family meal.

This contact also helps you keep an eye out for any issues your children may encounter as they continue to grow and mature. While you've loosened the reigns to help your kids experiment and enjoy their self-discovery, they are still dependent on you for formation. Regular communication will help you step in when they need you.

---

can be helpful to prepare yourself for these changes and to remind yourself about how you wanted to exercise your newfound freedom when you were young.

Your main goal when your children come home will be to determine whether the changes are harmful or if they are just a surprise. For example, it may surprise you to see your daughter or son sporting a new earring, face piercing, or hairstyle—but those things aren't really anything to be alarmed about. Young adulthood is the perfect time to explore a new look and a "new you." It's all part of the journey of growing up.

But if your children come home with a concerning weight change, mood disturbance, or obvious health issue, be aware that these are things that put them at risk. Because your children are not completely independent from you, you still need to step in to help guide them to healthier behaviors.

So, be prepared to be surprised. But also be prepared to take a closer look at how your young adult children are changing. You may have been in contact since they went away, but there is nothing like a sit-down family meal to assess how your children are doing.

Remember Those Nonnegotiables?

Every family has rules that still apply even as their children become completely independent. I'm talking about things such as respect, courtesy, and fidelity to important family traditions, such as regular meals and spiritual or religious obligations. Every family is different, and only you will know what the nonnegotiable rules are for your family.

If your young adults call aspects of your family's life and tradition into question, that is okay. Questioning why the family does something a certain way is part of their self-discovery. As long as the questioning is done with respect, it is done within the boundaries of your family rules. Respect is always a nonnegotiable.

Too Old for Discipline?

What if your young adult children don't respect your family's nonnegotiables? This is the question I get the most from parents of young adults, and the answer is pretty simple. Although every family has different rules, the response to disrespecting those rules is the same: have an adult conversation outlining why your children's behavior is not appropriate for the adults they want to become.

For example, courtesy is an integral family rule. If your child makes plans to have a family meal and then bails at the last minute or blows you off entirely, that shows a lack of courtesy. So, it is

Drama-Free Checklist

With only a few family meals a year, you may feel pressured to fix the world's (or at least the family's) problems over dinner. But remember:

- Keep solution-oriented conversations from the dinner table.
- Maintain an atmosphere that encourages conversation.
- Hold sensitive conversations during your one-on-ones.

perfectly reasonable to exercise discipline by explaining why that behavior is inappropriate and hurtful. Remember, discipline is all about learning, and this is an important life lesson!

Clarity of conversation and a tone of respect will help you have these discipline conversations with your young adults. Be aware that the way you talk about things, such as courtesy and respect, can either reinforce or contradict your nonnegotiables. Supper heroes who stay consistent with the character of their family have the highest success in disciplining young adults. Remember, no matter how old we are, we're all still students in life until we graduate to the afterlife.

If your kids become surprisingly disrespectful during this stage, go back and review the strategies outlined in chapter 5.

❷ **DID YOU KNOW?** Money is the main source of conflict between parents and adult children, according to 42 percent of the parents surveyed by Clark University.[31]

A Final Note

No matter how far away your young adults go in their journey of self-discovery, they won't be leaving the nest for good. Even the kids who go sprinting off toward independence with abandon make their way back home soon enough—that is, if you have created a welcoming environment. Keep your heart and mind open. My work has found that a healthy independence always leads to family togetherness!

---

[31] Jeffrey Jensen Arnett, *Parents and Their Grown Kids: Harmony, Support, and (Occasional) Conflict* (Worcester, MA: Clark University, 2013), 12, https://www2.clarku.edu/clark-poll-emerging-adults/pdfs/clark-university-poll-parents-emerging-adults.pdf.

EXERCISES

1. Nurture their independence.

    Why are your children still dependent on you? Make a list, and decide which thing makes the most sense to transfer over to them first. Then, based on how well your children handle the new responsibility, make a plan for transferring over the additional items on your list. As you did when they were younger, explain that this transfer isn't a burden; it is your way of helping them to become the adults they long to be.

2. Find your family's rules.

    You can't hold your young adults to all of the rules you had for them when they were children. But there are certain nonnegotiables you can enforce. Here is an easy way to define your family's rules.
    * Make a list of all the important rules you set for your children growing up.
    * Weed out all the rules that no longer apply.
    * Remove any items that are not integral to maintaining healthy family relationships.
    * Take a good hard look at the remaining items: these are your family rules.

3. Make time for family get-togethers.

    When your children were growing up, you created special meals. Now that they're grown up and moving out of the house, see how these special family meals overlap with school holidays, weekends, or other times when it may be more convenient to get together.

    Look for opportunities to get everyone home:
    * Seasonal holidays
    * Religious holidays
    * Secular holidays
    * Bank holidays
    * Birthdays
    * Anniversaries (wedding or even the anniversary of the death of a loved one)
    * Make up your own holiday!

4. Enjoy a special meal.

Celebrate your young adults' meals at home with something special: thirst-quenching shrimp dishes. These recipes (pages 124 and 125) also incorporate ingredients many young adults enjoy: wine and beer!

MISSION COMPLETE?

Strategies for Meals with Adult Children

When your children are completely self-supporting, financially stable, and fully capable of taking care of themselves *and* others, they've achieved independence! Your great mission is complete! Congratulations are in order. Break out the bubbly!

Seriously, take a deep breath and be grateful that you can now watch the fruits of your labor flourish and, hopefully, make you proud! In the growing quiet of your home, thankfully reflect on all the blessings you have received in helping your children get to this point. You've done a very wonderful thing—not just for your family, but for our larger human family.

You've successfully sent your children into the world to be their own supper heroes. And yet, just because the training wheels of young adulthood have been removed, that doesn't mean you're no longer a necessary part of your children's lives. They still very much need, and will always need, your ongoing love, encouragement, and support.

This new stage in your children's lives means only—and I'm sure you saw this coming—that you have to reconceptualize what it means to be a parent all over again. But take heart. This is the last time.

> ❷ **DID YOU KNOW?** Relationships improve during the adult years. According to a 2013 study by Clark University, 66 percent of parents get along better with their children after their teenage years. Adult children agreed, with 75 percent saying they get along better with their parents now than when they were teens.[32]

Taking a Back Seat

Up to this point, you have been like a farmer—planting, nurturing, and patiently waiting for the right time to harvest your crops. Now is that time. You have actively fed them everything they need to be independent. They are ready to separate from the vine. And, hard as it is, they are ready for you to take a more passive and supportive role so they can continue to learn and grow.

While your children learned a lot about independence as young adults, they always had you as a safety net. Now, as adults, they need to learn the life lessons that come with firsthand experience. The only way they can learn how to course-correct after a mistake, for example, or bounce back from a failure, is to face these things completely on their own, even though they are never alone.

Many of the parents I work with have trouble with this transition. I know how hard it is to see children head down a road that you know leads nowhere or struggle to learn a lesson you yourself learned the hard way. I can only imagine this is multiplied when they are your own kids! But there is no better feeling than seeing someone, no matter what his struggles, eventually stand on his own two feet.

You've Been Training for This

You've spent years paying attention to your growing family. You may even know your children better than they know themselves. Wisdom comes with years and experience, and you know what? You now have both!

So, while your primary role as supper hero is "done," being a parent isn't something you can retire from. It's just that instead of actively teaching your children, they are drawing on life lessons

---

[32] Arnett, *Parents and Their Grown Kids*, 8.

you imparted long ago. Or they are coming to you to discuss complicated problems and trusting the wisdom in the life experiences you share.

You're like that older, more patient wisdom figure every superhero needs! And you've been training for this your entire parental life! You may not realize it, but every life lesson you learned along the way has been lovingly cataloged somewhere. Now is the time to reflect on those lessons so you are ready when your adult children come to you for advice and guidance.

Eating Equal

As with meals with young adults, regular meals you have with your adult children need to be discussed and planned out in a manner that takes everyone's schedules into account. The main difference is that your children are now completely independent from you.

Before, while you were respecting your children's schedules, you could still lay down the law. Now, your children are your equals. They may even be supper heroes to their own children! You and your adult children are both equally independent people who are making equal efforts to stay connected as a family. Their true and complete independence has shifted the paradigm.

◄Œ FOOD FOR THOUGHT
Other New Roles

I know that many families face unique challenges that cause adult parents to take on additional new roles in this phase of their lives. I am always impressed by the tenacity and care I see in the people taking on new roles. These struggles are more common than you might think. The number of people raising their grandchildren is up 7 percent since 2009, and people taking care of aging parents is three times higher today than in 1998.* In every instance, regular meals help these modern families grow stronger and healthier, together. It also gives credibility to the idea that families need each other to be supper heroes for each other!

* Alejandra Cancino, "More Grandparents Raising Their Grandchildren," PBS NewsHour, February 16, 2016, https://www.pbs.org/newshour/nation/more-grandparents-raising-their-grandchildren; Glenn D. Braunstein, "Caring for Aging Parents Is Labor of Love—with a Cost," *Huffington Post*, April 15, 2013, https://www.huffingtonpost.com/glenn-d-braunstein-md/caregivers-aging-parents_b_3071979.html?ec_carp=2451359752813550844.

FAMILY STORY
Make Sure You've Got the Right Recipe Handy!

I was talking to a mother of adult children about how a supper hero's job is never done. She told me she always knows what recipe to reach for when her children all come home for a family meal. That's when it clicked!

Just as you want to have a family recipe handy for when all the children come home, you want it to be easy to turn to the right life lesson when you need it! Many parents have found that reflecting on past experience helps them draw on the right life lesson at the right time for their adult children.

In my work, I've discovered that the families who acknowledge this equality are the ones with a higher rate of success in continuing family meals. Respecting everyone's priorities equally translates into family meals that are easier to keep regular because the schedule makes sense for everyone—even if it means only three to five times a year.

❷ **DID YOU KNOW?** Parents and adult children see eye to eye. In a survey from Clark University, parents recorded the following as the biggest changes in their relationship with their children since their children were fifteen years old: 86 percent have more adult conversations; 78 percent enjoy their time together more; 71 percent are treated with more respect by their children; and 49 percent are treated more like another person than like a parent.[33]

Handing Off the Baton

A blessing of your new equal relationship is that you don't have to take on the burden of planning and cooking and doing everything yourself! You started the process of handing over mealtime responsibilities to your children during their teenage years. Complete that process now.

Put the ball firmly in your children's court. Hand off the baton by encouraging *them* to take responsibility for reaching out to *you*! Let them call you, take you out to eat, or cook a meal for you.

You helped them get to a place in their lives where they are able to serve you. Now give them the opportunity to do it. Let them experience being an equal with you in terms of love and

---

> FAMILY STORY
> ## My First Family Get-Together
> I remember when I first took the baton from my parents. I decided to have everyone over to celebrate my moving into my first apartment. It took some time to get everyone's schedules to align, but I coordinated the entire evening.
>
> The moment they walked into my home and saw the banquet I put out for them, I felt like a true equal with my parents. We were always equal in dignity, but now I felt as if we were equal in our ability to respond to life events — that we had equal responsibility.
>
> I felt like the adult my parents formed me to be. It was my turn to be the gracious host, to offer hospitality, and to encourage family togetherness. Now, family gatherings happen at my house and my siblings' houses quite regularly. It's one of the reasons why, despite all our dysfunctions, we can still say we are a close, loving family!

responsibility. Allow them to feel the joy of sharing what they have with those they love. It's your children's turn to hold the baton, to be the superhero!

What If They Won't Come Running to Me?

Putting the ball in our kids' court or giving them room to grow may not produce immediate results. We've talked about our culture's bias for immediate satisfaction. It is difficult to wait, especially when it comes to something as important as family, and you may feel as if your children will never come to you or that, when they do, it will be too late.

It's important to stick with it. Call on all that patience you developed stepping on toys you just put away or cleaning floors you just mopped! Your children will come to learn and understand the meaning of family togetherness with distance and time.

> ❷ **DID YOU KNOW?** Most parents worry about four main things. According to a survey from Clark University, parents have four main concerns about their adult children: financial problems (38 percent), making poor choices in romantic partners (28 percent), and lack of progress in their careers (27 percent) and in their education (26 percent).[34]

---

[34] Ibid., 13.

In my family, my older sister was a handful! But now that she's had time to grow and learn as an adult, she's always back at my mom and dad's home. The former rebel has become my parent's chauffeur, body guard, and, in many ways, best friend. I'm confident that all of my siblings feel the same way. I know this for a fact because I am my parents' favorite child (ha ha). As we've grown and matured, my siblings and I have developed a greater appreciation for all of our parent's sacrifices and everything they've done for us.

> ❷ **DID YOU KNOW?** Avoidance is never the answer. According to a 2009 study by Purdue and Pennsylvania State Universities, tensions between parents and adult children increase as the adult children age. The study found that this is due to parental concerns about their children's success and the multiple-role demands placed on middle-age children. In every case, avoidance of these issues didn't work and even appeared to make some conflicts worse.[35] So keep those lines of communication with your children open, and remember, a great place to do so is always around the table.

When Babies Have Babies

When parents become grandparents, or even great-grandparents, something incredible happens. I alluded to it at the beginning of this chapter. The supper-hero parents become wise guides for their supper-hero children. Often relieved of the day-to-day pressures of raising the kids, grandparents also have years of life experience that help them to be much more lenient, patient, and wonder-filled when interacting with their grandchildren.

This instinctual approach to formation is one of the many reasons I believe that healthy intergenerational relationships are so important. I know from my continued relationship with my grandmother that the practical logistics of regular intergenerational meals may require a good bit of coordination. But these hassles are trivial compared with the benefits your children receive from meaningful relationships with people of older generations.

We will discuss this further in chapter 10, but for now, I want to encourage you to give your children regular opportunities to interact with their grandparents as much as possible.

---

[35] Kira S. Birditt, Laura M. Miller, Karen L. Fingerman, and Eva S. Lefkowitz, "Tensions in the Parent and Adult Child Relationship: Links to Solidarity and Ambivalence," *Psychology and Aging* 24, no. 2 (June 2009), https://www.ncbi.nlm.nih.gov/pmc/articles/PMC2690709/.

Is the Job Ever Done?

The dynamics of the family are ever changing, but love, support, and fidelity remain essential even as your relationships transform and grow. And while family meals continue to evolve throughout life's stages, their regularity—again that could be just a few scheduled times each year—remains a powerful way to keep your family together.

More than the cement that keeps us all loving and growing together with each passing generation, regular family meals become a reminder of how we did not give in to the destructive tendencies of our society and watch our family grow apart.

EXERCISES

1. Pause and reflect.

   Now that your primary role as supper hero is complete, take some time to look back on all the things you learned. What would you tell another parent just starting out about how best to raise a family? Make a list of the top five things every parent should know. You may be sharing it with your own children soon.

2. Teach by example.

   Transitioning from being a driving force in your child's life to being a more contemplative or silent resource for them can be really hard. Think of some ways you can be active as a role model of good behaviors for your adult children.

3. Consider ways to hand off the baton.

   What are some things you can hand off to your children? You may be ready to unload, or you might want to keep doing the heavy lifting. That's up to you. Either way, identify real, tangible ways you can give your adult children the opportunity to contribute to family mealtime.

4. Be creative in scheduling regular family meals.

   If your family members live far apart, you need to work together to figure out how you can all stay connected while still feeling natural and not forced. Be creative, and consider technological advancements, such as video calling or live streaming events. Be bold, and think about opportunities outside the typical calendar celebrations. After all, it's the family togetherness that makes mealtimes special. There's no need to wait for a particular time of year. What are you waiting for? Get planning!

5. Try a recipe for two.

   If you're adjusting to cooking for two after your children have left home, try the cubed-steak recipes beginning on page 126. And give the recipe to your grown children who are starting out in cooking for themselves.

CHAPTER

9

MISSION CRITICAL

Continuing Regular Meals After
Your Children Have Flown the Coop

Without the kids at home, many parents feel as if they've lost their anchor. My parents struggled to redefine themselves without all the rushing around and caring for us kids. Change of this magnitude is challenging for every supper hero, but it can be especially strenuous when you are navigating these turbulent waters along with your spouse, who is going through the same struggle.

To avoid getting lost at sea, I like to remind families I work with that their children are the branches of their family tree, not its roots. You and your spouse have always been a team. You got through the terrible twos and the craziness of your children's teenage years together. Yes, family is the sum of its members, but the parents are the real anchor.

You and your spouse are the original "family." That means you can harness the power of regular family meals to help strengthen your family of two through your golden years.

➤ FOOD FOR THOUGHT

Think Back on Those First Meals

Take a moment to reflect on what it was like when you and your spouse started dating. Back then, it was just the two of you, and many of your dates were centered on meals! This is your opportunity to rekindle those memorable moments and make new memories with special meals—just for two.

What's So Golden About It?

With our society's fixation on youth, some may wonder what is so golden about this time of life. But when you think about it, gold is made when impurities are burned away from precious metal. Similarly, at this later stage in your life, you and your spouse have a second chance to focus on yourselves and your relationship, with the frivolities of youth removed.

This is not a selfish (or childish) time of transformation. It is truly an opportunity to move your needs as a couple to center stage once again, with a spirit of continually growing, learning, improving, and living. Of course, I believe the best place to do this work is at the dinner table.

Regular meals—daily, if possible—allow you and your partner to reap the same benefits that regular meals provided your children with. And just as F.O.O.D. (Fidelity, Obedience, Opportunity, and Discernment) was your guide to what to feed your children, my favorite four letter word can also guide your dinners with your spouse.

❷ **DID YOU KNOW?** Post-parenting is a mixed blessing for everyone. If you and your partner aren't feeling quite the same way about your empty nest, don't worry! Many parents face this stage of their lives with a different mix of feelings—but all are exciting in their own way: 75 percent feel as if "anything is possible"; 67 percent find it "a fun and exciting time"; 59 percent see it as a time to find out who they really are; and 71 percent experience a great deal of freedom.[36]

Family Meals Continued

Regular family meals have always been an avenue for you to show your *fidelity* to your family. In recent years, however, you were probably more focused on showing your children, rather than your spouse, how committed you are. Now is the time to shift your focus.

---

[36] Arnett, *Parents and Their Grown Kids*, 27.

Just as family meals helped to send a message of fidelity to your children, they can help you share that same message with your spouse. Keeping family meals after your children have gone reinforces your dedication. It shows that the time together wasn't just for the kids; it was for your spouse too.

Your commitment to each other becomes increasingly important as you transition from active to passive supper heroes and redefine your familial relationships. Actively continuing to build and strengthen your fidelity to your partner is also a positive lesson for your adult children. And in keeping the foundation of your family strong, you are ultimately helping the entire family grow stronger.

What's Your Relationship Status?

When children come into the picture, many couples transform from their original dream team into a parental tour de force. After their kids grow up and leave the nest, however, Mom and Dad can remain stuck in parent mode. The hole caused by their children's absence may cause parents of adult children to feel like something is missing in their relationship with their partner.

Through my work, I've learned that it is often hard for couples experiencing this transition to articulate exactly how they feel. That is why obedience is such a great way to lean on your spouse for support during this transitional time. When we discussed obedience in chapter 3, we talked about the Latin root of the word, which means "to listen." We also discussed how obedience requires humility to listen to the truths others have to share.

Many couples I work with who have used dinner discussions to explore where they are with their spouses say that it has helped them immensely in handling the transition. By truly listening to what the other has to share, couples are able to navigate the transition as a team. They end up moving through the challenge together, growing stronger as individuals and as a couple.

FAMILY STORY
He Was Too Scared to Ask

Many couples I've worked with come to me because they've let the family meal lapse. I remember one husband who was very nervous about asking his wife to start having regular family meals again. We talked about his fears, and he agreed to have a conversation with his wife.

The next time I saw him, he had a huge grin on his face! His wife thought it was a fantastic idea. All the fear and apprehension he had was self-made. His wife was excited and eager to start having regular meals again.

> **❓ DID YOU KNOW?** Happy couples talk more. A study showed that people who spend five hours or more talking together each week have the most successful marriages.[37] Adding up daily dinner conversations gets you to five plus hours pretty quickly. Coincidence? I think not!

Keeping Your Married Life Spicy

My second book, *Spicing Up Married Life*, is all about making sure couples take every opportunity to keep their marriage strong. Although the book drew on my years providing Pre-Cana courses and my experience counseling couples facing a range of critical issues, I also explored how the dinner table is a great place for couples to strengthen their relationship.

While you are continuing regular meals without your children, it's important not to fall into a routine. You want to keep yourself and your spouse feeling excited about your time together. To do so, you need to continue to challenge each other, and to give each other new opportunities to grow, just as you gave your children such opportunities.

One way to keep things spicy is to create special meals throughout the year. You don't have to wait to celebrate your love on your anniversary or on Valentine's Day. Celebrate it regularly, as my book suggests. Create a "month-aversary," with a special night each month! Isn't that what you've wanted all those years you spent changing diapers and cleaning mashed peas off your walls? Now you have the opportunity to spend more time together. Seize it!

> **❓ DID YOU KNOW?** Couples who have new experiences are more satisfied. According to Arthur Aron of the Interpersonal Relationships Lab at Stony Brook University in New York, couples who do new things together are more satisfied in their marriage.[38]

These moments can be anything from trying out a new recipe to trying out a new restaurant. Anything that gives you and your beloved companion something new and fun to look forward to, do it. Be as creative as when you first met. In fact, that's a great dinner idea: recreate your first date! Call on the ingenuity you employed to get your children to eat broccoli.

---

[37] Melanie Pinola, "This Infographic Reveals the Secrets of the Happiest Couples," LifeHacker, February 7, 2014, https://lifehacker.com/this-infographic-reveals-the-secrets-of-the-happiest-co-1518305669.

[38] Arthur Aron et al., "Couples' Shared Participation in Novel and Arousing Activities and Experienced Relationship Quality," *Journal of Personality and Social Psychology* 78, no. 2 (February 2000): 273–284, http://dx.doi.org/10.1037/0022-3514.78.2.273.

I cannot stress enough how important I think it is that we all keep our lives spicy, never boring, and that we work on living each day as if it were our last. Your kids, now very established in their lives, still have a lot to learn from you. How much they are able to learn depends on whether you're willing to show them how much life there is yet to live.

Dinner Discussions

As always, the dinner table is the perfect place to discern through meaningful dinner conversations. Now that your children are grown, however, there's no need to have separate personal conversations away from the dinner table. So, although fewer voices may be contributing to the dialogue, you now have the freedom to talk about anything and everything that's important to you.

In addition to examining the challenges of the parental transition, talk about what you both want out of your golden years. Challenge each other to try new things. Support each other's dreams. Take the time to explore and to support each other. This is your opportunity to take back your dinner discussions and dig into the topics you really want to talk about.

Remember, you're never too old to learn about your spouse or yourself. Get excited and get ready! These more regular, meaningful conversations with just your spouse provide a taste of the supper hero's victory!

FAMILY STORY

Keepin' It Spicy

I dedicated *Spicing Up Married Life* to my parents and released the book on their fiftieth wedding anniversary. They laughed and questioned what they could learn from this book after fifty years of marriage. But that book, like this one, wasn't written to teach anything new. It was written to help people practice their primary responsibility, which is to love one another, and to love each day of life as a special gift from God.

After my mom and dad read the book, they admitted, "Son, it's a good book," with rather mischievous smiles on their faces. Yup, I think they took the book's purpose to heart. They didn't need me to teach them, but perhaps a little priestly encouragement reminded them that raising their children wasn't their only responsibility. They still had to work on loving one another and on making the most of every day.

FAMILY STORY
Turn Off the TV

At a couples retreat, I asked the couple who had been married the longest, sixty years, if I could ask them some questions. They had a lot of great advice, but when I asked the wife what she wanted to tell her husband but never had, she said she wished he'd turn off the TV when they have dinner together. He didn't realize she wanted to talk during dinner and was glad to turn it off for them to have more time together. It was a complete eye-opener for them as a couple.

EXERCISES

1. See your nest as half full.

   An empty home isn't an empty life! Think about what you are excited about tackling now that you have more time and energy to focus on your interests. What is something you want to do for yourself or for your marriage? Discuss it with your spouse over your next dinner.

2. Go out on a date.

   Dates are purposeful opportunities to celebrate each other and to learn more about each other (and yourselves). So, make time to do something special. Go out to a new restaurant or try out a new recipe. Think up at least three things you can do this month to add some more spice to your loving relationship with your spouse.

3. Try something new.

   It's never too late to teach an old dog new tricks! What are some foods you've never tried? While you may not have an interest in trying that food, go ahead and be adventurous. If finding a new restaurant is tough in your part of the world, head to the Internet and get a new recipe from another country or culture.

4. Be a kid at heart.

   It's easy to let the world pass by and feel as if we're just observers. But we're supposed to live each day to the fullest. What are some activities you can get into? If you have a bad hip, you probably shouldn't try climbing Mount Kilimanjaro. But you sure could take up an art class, join a book club, or enter a local baking competition! How can you become a kid at heart by getting excited by a hobby or a craft?

5. Cook a spicy meal for two.

Try the Bourbon Salmon for Two (see the recipe on page 130) for a delicious, nutritious dish with a bourbon glaze that will spice up your meal!

GENERATIONS OF SUPPER HEROES UNITE!

The Importance of Intergenerational Meals

So far, we've discussed regular meals with your children as they grow up, meals with your adult children, meals with your children's children, and meals with your spouse. But what about regular meals with your parents?

In the whirlwind of today's modern life, many families I work with seem to overlook these "extra" people who make up the family. But children who grow up not knowing their grandparents often have no desire to start a relationship with them later in life. With no time invested in intergenerational bonding, the branches of the family tree split apart.

Weak intergenerational relationships rob younger generations of the benefits of interacting with their elders, and vice versa. This causes the family as a whole to weaken. The good news? There is a great place to have meaningful interactions between generations to keep this gap from growing. Now, where do you suppose that is?

Now, I know what you're thinking: "Father Leo, I barely have time to eat with my children and my spouse. How am I ever going to work in additional meals that get my parents—and my spouse's parents—around the dinner table with us?" To answer that, let's reflect on everything we learned in chapter 4.

Regular means something different for each family. All you really have to do (and I know I am making this sound easier than it is) is schedule meals with a sense of dependable consistency. Remember, although it may not feel like it, we are the masters of our schedules. We can set our lives up in a way that gives priority to the things that matter to us most, such as our extended family.

Regular intergenerational meals could be scheduled once every other month, or if your parents or in-laws live farther away, it could only be a handful of times a year. (As a rule, I find it's best to have meals with grandparents more than just once a year.) If distance is a barrier, try to schedule digital dinner dates. Really. It surprised me at first, but many grandparents are much more technologically savvy than we think. And many are motivated to learn more about technology to connect with their grandkids.

Setting places at the table and having your parents join you via video call may be the technological solution you need to make regular intergenerational meals work for your family. At the end of the day, it's not how you get the meals to happen; it's just that you have them regularly.

---

[39] Alliance for Children and Families, *Intergenerational Family Connections: The Relationships That Support a Strong America* (Washington, D.C.: Alliance for Children and Families, 2014), 4.
[40] Ibid., 5.

Start 'em Young

It's always easiest to start a tradition when children are young. It may not feel like it at the time, but doing the hard work of setting up intergenerational meals when the kids are little establishes a routine that often self-perpetuates into the future. If you start intergenerational meals early, they may just keep on churning — even as life gets increasingly complicated.

Interactions with older generations are very important for your children early on in their development. This is the time when they form foundational ideas about the world around them that will guide them for the rest of their lives. Intergenerational relationships give children a sense of where they came from, as well as an understanding of where many of the traditions and beliefs you hold as an immediate family originated.

Another fundamental lesson young children learn is how older people should be treated. This is why it is so important that we always treat the elderly with patience and care. After all, that is how we will want them to treat us.

> ➤ FOOD FOR THOUGHT
> ### No Time Like the Present
> While intergenerational meals, like most family traditions, are easier to start when your children are young, there is no time like the present. Your teenagers, young adult children, and adult children still look to you for what is important for the family. You are their foundation, their rock. If you express and show by your actions that connecting with people of the older generation is important, that is often enough for them to follow your lead.

Keep It Going

Even if your child started interacting with older generations early, it is important that you continue doing your best to strengthen these relationships as your children age into adulthood. Maintain regular meals with your parents and in-laws, and encourage your maturing children to do so as well. Eventually, you will want to transfer responsibility for these relationships over to your adult children.

The lessons your children learn about older generations when they are young will be enriched as they age. Continued meals together also provide new opportunities for growth. Intergenerational dinner conversations, for example, breathe life into recent history, enable younger generations to appreciate their heritage, and reinforce all that previous generations contributed.

FAMILY STORY

Continuing Meals with Grandma Patalinghug

As I write this book, my grandmother has lived a long time—one hundred years! Despite my absolutely crazy schedule, I fly out to see her every Christmas. It's not just because I love her very much (or because I'm her favorite grandchild, wink, wink) but also because my fidelity to family makes me want to learn how to care for its elderly members.

One year, I heard that she was having difficulty eating meals, so I decided to get her a special gift to help her eat all her puréed foods (which my relatives make fresh and delicious, by the way). I gave her a plate with the image of Jesus' face on it and told her that she has to eat all her vegetables in order to see Jesus. It has become her favorite thing! She eats now. It's not a miracle. It's love!

Frankly, seeing her and seeing how she is cared for keeps me grounded, humbled, and anchored. It reminds me that no matter how busy I am, I need to take time to spend with people I love.

Keep your eyes open, and encourage your children to keep theirs open as well. There are lots of opportunities for children to help and teach their grandparents.

What If It's Just Not in the Cards?

I realize that every family is different and there are unique circumstances. Some people's parents have passed away. Others have reasons for being irreconcilably estranged. In every case, however, there is a way to bring regular interactions with older generations into your children's lives. And you should, because these intergenerational relationships are critical to your child's formation.

If your parents and your spouse's parents are not available, you can always form a connection with someone from an older generation who shares your values. These relationships can supplement a biological grandparent by passing on to your children many of the benefits of intergenerational relationships, such as respect for older generations and the heritage of shared values.

I've met several people who have forged such strong bonds with older couples that they become, in effect, their children's surrogate grandparents.

Here's the Good News

You may be reading this chapter with a little knot growing in your stomach. Maybe you've made excuses not to see your in-laws or let distance grow between you and your parents. Maybe you didn't grow up knowing your grandparents and have no idea where to start. The good news is that there are things you can start doing today to begin building intergenerational relationships.

If you are blessed to have the opportunity to reconnect your children to their grandparents, do it. Don't wait until a holiday. Schedule a dinner, lunch, breakfast, or brunch — but start building toward regular meals. You can also look for opportunities for your children to spend one-on-one time with their grandparents. Hey! You may have just found the perfect babysitter for your next "month-a-versary" date with your spouse!

Whatever path forward makes the most sense for your family, I really want to encourage you to take the first step toward building strong intergenerational relationships today. This is a challenge for many families. It can help to remember that you are showing your fidelity by feeding the generation that fed you!

> ❓ **DID YOU KNOW?** The first Sunday after Labor Day is Grandparents Day! We don't celebrate Grandparents' Day as a culture the same way we do with Father's Day and Mother's Day, or even Administrative Professionals' Day! Up to 66 percent of grandparents have never celebrated Grandparents Day![41] I'd like to challenge you to celebrate Grandparents Day this year — not in a commercialistic way, but just as a reminder to schedule a regular meal. Celebrate with gusto! And don't limit that celebrating to the national holiday.

EXERCISES

1. Good Cop Bad Cop

   It's easy for grandparents to be the "good cops" who allow grandchildren to stay up a little later and eat a few more cookies. Then the parents become the "bad cops" who have to enforce the rules they set forth. One of the best ways to avoid this duality of disciplines is simply to have a conversation with the grandparents, especially when it comes to very specific disciplinary topics. Consider the following ways to help divert the possible "cop-out" when it comes to discipline.

---

[41] "Surprising Facts about Grandparents," *Considerable*, August 12, 2009, https://considerable.com/surprising-facts-about-grandparents/.

- *Create a list of the nonnegotiables*, and make sure the grandparents are on the same page when it comes to enforcing the discipline.
- *Reflect on your experiences*, and make a mental list of all the ways your grandparents were more lenient or stricter with you. Then have a conversation with the grandparents, reflecting about what worked and what could have been improved upon.
- *Think ahead*: If you were a grandparent, how would you want to "spoil" your grandchildren? The fact is, being a grandparent is just as much of a goal as raising healthy children. It's a continuation of family traditions and shows how your experience has brought you to a powerful position, with a privilege to "spoil" your grandkids!

2. At mealtime, keep individual needs in mind.

   If you have family members who need softer foods, such as rice, try serving Mushroom Risotto or Chocolate Rice Porridge for an intergenerational meal. These recipes (pages 131 and 133) remind me of my own grandparents!

DIFFICULT DINNER DISCUSSION

Tackling Those Topics That Aren't Meant for the Dinner Table

Difficult dinner discussions happen. Yes, the Shiitake mushrooms inevitably hit the fan! But challenges, either from inside or outside our families, should never tear us apart. As your family's superhero supper hero, it's your job to use difficult dinner discussions to bring your family closer together rather than letting them drive your family apart.

To help you with this seemingly impossible task, I've pulled together my advice for addressing topics the families I work with face most often. I hope this summary can help your family tackle these challenging subjects. I look forward to more discussions with you and others about how we can all stop family food from turning into a family feud.

Handling Age Gaps

When families have multiple age groups, it can be extra challenging to find a topic that everyone enjoys. In my studies on communication, I've found that a spirit of generosity in listening to another person is the key to all good conversation. Model this behavior for your children and encourage them to do the same, no matter what the topic is.

If one child dominates the dinner conversation night after night, it may make sense for you to institute a schedule in which each member of the family takes turns coming up with a topic of conversation. The key is to pay attention. See who is participating in dinner and who is missing out on important formation. Then make the adjustments that make the most sense for your crew.

Bad Performance

Every family will experience a bad report card, a letter sent home from school, lies, and more. Even yours truly got caught taking my brother's quarters to play video games at the local convenience store (yes, I just dated myself). It's important to remember that these things are not the end of the world.

Many of these problems are just part of growing up and are truly not the big deal they feel like at the moment. Because regular family meals are dependent on the dinner table being welcoming, scolding should never happen there. In fact, I believe wasting moments of family fellowship in anger is a greater crime than any failing grade.

That's not to say you shouldn't discipline your children for misbehavior. It is very important to explain the impact of bad performance and even provide punishment if necessary. This just shouldn't be done at the table. If the "problem" must be addressed during the meal, do so briefly, setting a time and a place for further discussion. Then quickly bring the focus back to enjoying the time together as a family.

Don't let one bad apple spoil the bunch. Simply set it aside, and later turn it into apple butter instead.

Conflicting Beliefs

Children often develop different viewpoints from their parents, especially during their exploratory teenage years. Even if they don't, they will most certainly meet someone who has a different viewpoint during the course of their lives. How they handle these interactions begins with what they learn at home around the dinner table as their foundation.

Instead of letting emotions take the lead during these conversations, call on your humility, and encourage a conversation that explores your child's differing perspective. Do some research on the topic and bring that knowledge to future conversations to help your child continue to explore what he believes about the topic in light of all the facts.

Relying on science, statistics, and research helps diffuse emotions because it brings a sense of rationality and civility to the discussion. This approach lets your conversation be an exchange of ideas rather than a shouting match. Encourage your children to use these strategies whenever they encounter conflicting beliefs in their daily lives.

■■€ FOOD FOR THOUGHT

What About Politics?

Politics can get us very fired up. I've found success in trying to see both sides of every issue. In learning the facts, I help myself not get whisked away in the drama of the news cycle. I am also able to engage with people of all political beliefs. The truth is that the country will be only as strong as its citizens' understanding of what it means to be unified. And that unity starts in the family.

Relationships outside the Family

Whether it's with a boyfriend, girlfriend, best friend, or acquaintance—you want to make sure your children are pursuing relationships that bring out the best in them. If their relationships are damaging or impairing good decision-making skills, you are in for another difficult discussion.

Don't Focus Only on Problems

Often our focus is taken up by a problem we think we need to solve. This could be a teenager acting out or a toddler who has discovered that he's really good at throwing his broccoli. Whatever the case, if one child is dominating your attention during mealtime, you may want to set some time aside for your other children; maybe a study-break snack or a late-night cup of tea. This will give you more time to pay attention to needs you may not see on the surface.

I encourage families to start the conversation about positive relationships early. Instead of waiting to have a difficult discussion, devote a dinner to what positive relationships look like. Then encourage your children to embody those characteristics and to look for them in others. As your children age, provide gentle reminders of the types of relationships they agreed are best for them.

If your child is already in a relationship you are concerned about, gently discuss what good relationships are and why this one might be hurtful. Then discuss what could be changed. If this initial conversation is fruitless, try a more serious one-on-one discussion away from the dinner table. Don't be afraid to talk to your child's friend as well. It's important to see this as an opportunity for both of them to grow up, while recognizing how they are still in "formation" with a lot to learn.

Watch Out!

Unhealthy relationships can be hard to spot. Keep an eye out for tragic cases in which the relationship is unhealthy and all-consuming. Pay attention to outward signs such as weight gain or loss, lack of sleep, difference in dress, a bad attitude, and lack of attention to family members. These situations may require you or a professional to step in.

Making Difficult Decisions

Kids often want to use mealtime to ask permission to do things. Many parents I work with provide a gut response, which gets them into trouble, because it inevitably leads to a million follow-ups if the kids don't get the answer they want. "Because I said so," is a tempting strategy, but it doesn't reflect the mature adult you are helping your child grow into.

I encourage families to avoid this situation by establishing a rule that all permission questions need to be asked well in advance of when the decision needs to be made. Let your children know that this is because you need time to explore the issue thoroughly to determine what is best for your family.

In other words, punting to another time gives you room to think and an opportunity to regroup with your spouse to create a unified, thoughtful response. This approach also reinforces for your children the importance of discernment and the fact that decisions made on behalf of one person also impact others. Also, keep track of no versus yes responses, and seek a balance.

Bettering the Bullies

Unfortunately, another early conversation you need to have with your children is about bullying. This complicated and pervasive issue impacts so many children. I myself was bullied at school. Talk to your children about how they can be the best version of themselves regardless of what other people say. Use bullying as an opportunity to discuss your children's strengths and how they can best deal with the shortcomings of others.

Moral Discussions

Your children are going to face a lot of moral discussions and challenges, many while they are living under your roof. Start the conversation early by explaining that morality is all about seeking a life directed toward truth and goodness. Instead of stating certain things are wrong or bad, explore how each moral decision fits into the bigger picture. This often sounds less judgmental, which is key when exploring options with a maturing teenager.

Once again, information gathering is key. Arming your children with facts, while patiently encouraging them toward what is good and true, will help them make informed moral decisions. This is a tough topic, but dealing with it head-on can help your family mature in their understanding of morality and become forces of good and truth in this very immoral world.

FAMILY STORY

What if My Child Is the Bully?

I have met many families with children who act out and bully others in their attempt to work through issues in their lives. So please don't waste energy feeling terrible if you recognize bullying characteristics in your own child. Get right to work, starting difficult discussions that will encourage more positive behaviors. Bullying demonstrates personal insecurity.

One-on-one conversations are best here. Start by seeing if you can find out what's making your child act out aggressively. Then help him discern how he can make better choices, and encourage him to do so. Reassure your child that he can change. It all starts with an attitude of humility and making up with the people he treated poorly.

Sex and Sexuality

This topic may seem out of place for a dinner conversation, simply because talking about sex and sexuality *isn't* dinner conversation. But parents know that it *is* a topic that needs to be addressed.

This section is simply meant to give you a perspective on how to discuss this sensitive topic—away from the dinner table.

I've never understood why people in our sex-crazed culture have trouble talking to their kids about sex. Many of the parents I work with come to me in a panic when they have to have the dreaded birds-and-bees talk. I usually go over the basics, which are pretty self-explanatory, and then tell them they shouldn't think of "the talk" as a one-and-done deal. There are a lot of important topics to cover. In addition to the birds and the bees, it's crucial to talk to our young people about sex as a language. It can communicate positive messages of love or harmful messages of manipulation, depending on how it's used. It is also crucial to explain that sex is a gift—never a right. Without these distinctions, many kids grow up thinking that love is communicated with only one part of the body—and I'm not talking about the heart!

It's also important to encourage a healthy understanding of good physical touching and age-appropriate expressions of intimacy.

Helpful and Healthy Sex Checklist

Here's an easy way to see if you have a healthy moral attitude toward sex.*

- Faithful: Does sex communicate your commitment to your spouse?
- Free: Is sex engaged in without pressure of any kind?
- Fruitful: Does sex lead to goodness, and is it open to the gift of life?
- Total: Are you entirely focused on your spouse, or do you hold some secret from your spouse?

Finally, without sounding as if sex is bad, be sure also to discuss the consequences of sexual activity. Be clear about the realities of your child's actions in terms of sexually transmitted diseases and pregnancy.

* This teaching comes from St. John Paul II's Theology of the Body, which is explained by many apologists, including Christopher West. See Christopher West, "A Basic Theology of Marriage," Crossroads Initiative, https://www.crossroadsinitiative.com/media/articles/basic-theology-of-marriage-christopher-west/.

Finances

Many people have trouble discussing finances with their families. In my experience, parents who talk with their family about money in a fearless and appropriate way raise children who have a stronger sense of financial stability and gratitude. The best place to start is with the idea of wants versus needs. Instill in your children gratitude for what they have. A great way to do this, as we've mentioned in previous chapters, is to say "thank you" for the meal or offer a prayer before you eat.

Another important discussion to have is about the value and dignity of work. The provider for your family works incredibly hard to provide stability. This requires great sacrifice. At the same time, be careful not to inflict the strain of financial burden onto your children's tiny shoulders. One way to do this is to have a discussion dedicated to all the things money can't buy.

If your family is navigating financial difficulties, be sure to inject a healthy dose of optimism and an attitude of perseverance into your discussions. Yes, most of us have to make sacrifices to survive. Don't be afraid of it, and don't "give up" on your dreams of being financially stable. Show your family how creativity and collaboration can help you meet your needs.

Faith

Teaching your children about faith can start at a young age. It's best done when *both* parents take faith seriously. Discuss what you believe as a family and answer any questions your young children have about these beliefs. Provide a good foundation, but know that your children may still grow to believe something different—which is where the difficult discussions lie.

Each family will have different conversations about faith based on what they believe. In every situation, however, humility and a sense of humor make these difficult discussions easier. Remember, a common definition of *faith* is belief without proof. We don't have any hard facts for these discussions. We have to rely on each other to explore what we

FAMILY STORY

"I Think My Child's Religion Is Harming Her"

An atheist once came to me because his daughter joined a "cult." It turned out this was just how he saw the Catholic convent, where his daughter became a happy nun for many, many years. That being said, it's one thing when your children's views differ from yours. It's another when what they believe is harmful. Like healthy relationships, faith should never cause your children harm. If it does, you may need to get involved or request the help of a leader in your faith or another professional.

FOOD FOR THOUGHT

Regular Family Meals in Divorce

Regular meals after a divorce reinforce a sense of commitment and togetherness, even though someone is missing. If possible, try to bring your separated family together for a regular meal at least once a year. This can help your children's understanding of family fidelity, even if there's no longer the same commitment between the parents. I've counseled a divorced couple to do this, and they are happier knowing that they have learned to continue to love one another. Their family is still "saved," even if not under one roof.

believe, meaning that families can benefit greatly by learning about their personal faith together. Sometimes it is also necessary to remind ourselves of that quote from the movie *Rudy*, "There is a God, and I am not Him!"

Marital Problems and Divorce

I wish these particular dinner discussions never came up, but we all know they do. Marriage provides different challenges to every couple. Many couples come to me with very serious problems. The good news is that regardless of marriage's ups and downs, there are healthy ways for the family to deal with even the hardest marital difficulties.

The best advice I can give on this issue is not to use the dinner table as a place to air spousal problems. Doing so destroys the environment needed for regular family meals and provides a horrible example to your children. Just don't do it. That's not to say you shouldn't work on your problems. I greatly encourage you to do so and even to seek outside help if it is needed. Just don't destroy the foundation that a family dinner provides—even if it is a struggle. We all have to learn how to eat with people we may be angry with.

In addition, unless there are extreme extenuating circumstances, divorce doesn't mean that you and your spouse can't treat each other with respect for the good of the family. It may be extremely difficult or the last thing you want to do, but it is important to remember that a breakup is not about just two people; it's about an entire family.

For young children, discuss how problems with your spouse have no relation to your enduring love for them. If you are divorced, do your best to explain that you simply don't have the kind of love for your ex-spouse necessary for marriage. When your children get a little older, humbly discuss those things that you believe led to your marriage ending. Transform your life lessons into opportunities for your children to learn about love, marriage, and maturity.

Trying Times

Things out of our control will happen. Sickness, death, job loss, stock market crashes—the list is endless. In these trying times, the power of the family meal really shows itself. Mealtime becomes the bedrock that strengthens each member's resolve to live life with a sense of hope and purpose, no matter what challenges come.

The dinner table can be the place where people realize they are *not* alone. Eating together, even if it's at a hospital, is a great sign of fidelity. Even if you aren't saying anything, you're all communicating your love and who you are to each other just by serving each other and being with each other. Bread shared with others becomes a form of culinary consolation.

Preparing a family meal can be a very healthy and positive distraction during difficult times because it serves a purpose. It can also be helpful to serve others. Often when we think we have it tough, other people can remind us that the greatest challenges in our lives are not as bad as what others are dealing with.

And companionship, with bread shared with others, becomes a form of culinary consolation.

When the Dust Settles

After a particularly difficult dinner discussion, it's important to remind the family that a conversation is just a sharing of ideas and opinions. The family that talks through these difficult issues together emerges stronger and better for it. The power of food and family help us become stronger and better able to digest the bitter herbs of reality.

I know you can handle any difficult discussion that comes your way. Just be patient with yourself. Don't try to rush a solution for every challenge. You won't always have all the answers. But you will have many more dinners ahead of your family if you navigate these difficult issues instead of avoiding them.

It is going to get hot in the kitchen for sure, but in the madness and rush of it all, I know you can create a masterpiece of lifelong lessons for you and your family. (You can also create a delicious dessert that uses heat to complement a semisweet chocolate mousse. See the recipe on page 134.)

EXERCISE

1. Ask!

   I know there are even more difficult discussions. This is just a summary of the topics I've encountered in my twenty-plus years of priesthood and family ministry. But I know one thing: the people who get the help are those who ask. So, I ask you: Are there any difficult discussion topics that are not included? Feel free to reach out to me by email at assistant@fatherleofeeds.com or on my social media platforms to ask me any further questions you may have. The goal is to help you break open the difficult discussions and reach the hearts of those you love, so I will seek to offer any perspective or opinion I have about those stifling conversations. As I said from the start, consider me a companion. Sharing meals means you are never alone!"

THE WORLD NEEDS MORE SUPPER HEROES

How Feeding Others Can Change the World

Imagine that you are starving—not just hungry, but starving. People around you are eating, and worse, wasting food. You long for something to eat, but they don't share with you.

Unfortunately, that's the reality of our world today. Even people in modern and developed nations, where there's not a lack of food, sit quietly or with a flimsy sign that silently screams "I need help!" Yes, some are scammers, but many more go hungry every day because we are not feeding each other as we should. I say "we" because even though I've made feeding the hungry a priority in my life, I know that I can be doing more. With hundreds of millions of people undernourished

SAVING THE FAMILY

globally,[42] we can all be doing more to end world hunger. In fact, I know that if we all work together, we can feed the roughly one in nine people who go hungry every day.

Why Feeding Others Is So Important

I believe strongly in feeding the hungry because it is a simple act that has the power to save the entire world. Talk about a supper hero's duty! Many people look at me strangely when I start talking like this about feeding others. How can an act so small change the entire world? Well, I think the following story illustrates my point quite well.

One day, a man dies and finds himself at a grand feast. Everything about it looks like the paintings he has seen of heaven. There is a large banquet table with bright white lights, harps, togas—the works. The man goes to eat the food in front of him, but he can't! The utensils are too long, and no matter how hard he tries, he can't put any of the food in his mouth. After a while, he begins to starve. That's when he realizes he isn't in heaven; he's in hell!

The crazy thing is the man was right about the banquet hall being the exact same as the one in heaven. Every physical detail about the hall in hell was a carbon copy of the one in heaven. The only difference is that no one goes hungry in heaven because everyone there uses those long utensils to feed each other.

When we make feeding each other a priority, we may be changing only one small thing about the world, but in doing so we are changing everything. We are changing, and I believe saving, the world!

❓ **DID YOU KNOW?** For Catholics, food has a deeper meaning. For Catholics, the Presence of Jesus and His Body and Blood are contained in the bread and wine. Catholics believe that, by eating, digesting, and receiving nourishment from the Presence of Jesus in the Eucharist, they will become more like Jesus, who feeds hungry hearts and souls.

My Calling to Feed the Flock

I am just a man who has freely and lovingly chosen to become a priest in order to "feed the flock." This is my calling in life. It's why I became a priest and why I became a chef. I have dedicated

---

[42] Food and Agricultural Organization of the United States, *The State of Food Security and Nutrition in the World* (Rome: Food and Agricultural Organization of the United States, 2018), 6.

my life to that part in the Gospel of John in which Jesus basically says, "If you love me, feed my sheep" (see John 21:17).

Be Generous with Your Attention

You can't give money to everyone who asks, but you can still be generous to those in need. I think it's a great practice to keep food in your car or something small like a granola bar in your pocket to hand out. Even if you think that you don't have anything to give, however, you can always give your attention. If I can't help someone, I always try to look the person in the eye and say, "I'm sorry, I can't help at this time." I make it a point to be generous with my attention, and to remember those individuals in heartfelt prayer. I believe that giving attention is just as important as anything else, and it's important that we remember to give it generously.

---

❷ **DID YOU KNOW?** Jesus was challenging His followers in Luke 10:8. His instruction "Whenever you enter a town and they receive you, eat what is set before you" was easier said than done for His followers. This is because many of Jesus' followers were Jewish and, by Jewish law, had very strict dietary observations. I believe, however, that Jesus was trying to tell His followers (including me) that the best place to develop friendship and an eventual sense of "family" togetherness is at the dinner table.

Of course, feeding people is about more than just physical food. As we've discussed in previous chapters, feeding people is all about F.O.O.D. (Fidelity, Obedience, Opportunity, and Discernment). To provide people with what they need, I believe that you have to meet them where they are. Be a part of their lives. Share what you have with them, and be willing to receive what they share in return, as Jesus said: "Whenever you enter a town and they receive you, eat what is set before you" (Luke 10:8).

Truly understanding Jesus' instructions about feeding others gave me a great foundation and helped me to understand what my liturgy should be. While the word *liturgy* is typically used to describe a church service today, it comes from the Greek word for "work." I like to remember that when considering my liturgy, because I take my work of feeding Jesus' flock very seriously.

►◄ FOOD FOR THOUGHT

Beating Swords into Plowshares

This topic always gets me thinking about Isaiah 2:4: "He shall judge between the nations, / and shall decide for many peoples; / and they shall beat their swords into plowshares, / and their spears into pruning hooks; / nation shall not lift up sword against nation, / neither shall they learn war any more."

Those who claim to be Catholic but exclude people from God's love are obviously forgetting what the Catholic Faith is all about. It's similar to the way some people forget we are part of the human family. It's important that we never forget this universal truth.

Faith without Works

Many people I talk with believe that we should feed the hungry. Passionate individuals tell me that they donate money to local charities or run food drives and do many wonderful charitable works! You don't need money, however, to be able to help contribute to your larger human family. The possibilities are endless, especially when you remember to be generous with your attention and with your time.

My calling to feed the hungry has led me to many amazing places. It all started with Grace Before Meals, now known as Plating Grace. When I started, I had no idea that it would grow into the international movement it is today. I just wanted a way to help families come back to the dinner table. In fact, I am continually humbled that so many different types of people are joining the movement.

Traveling around the world as a part of Plating Grace and my food-and-faith movement, I was blessed with the opportunity to work with many families. This gave me a new understanding of the undeniable benefits of regular family meals. Listening to what people around the world hunger for, I saw for the first time how hungry the world is for supper heroes!

This realization led me to start The Table Foundation, a nonprofit that seeks to elevate culture and family life through the universal language of a meal served with love. In addition to feeding the body, The Table Foundation works to feed the mind and the soul with those things it hungers for.

As I continued traveling across the globe, I met a number of wonderful organizations all working to "feed the hungry" in different ways. One of these groups, Chefs for Peace, includes Christian, Jewish, and Muslim chefs who promote unity and fellowship through food. I joke they can work together because they have really sharp knives, but their true faith actually transforms what could be weapons into instruments they can use to serve one another lovingly!

These are just some of the countless individuals I have met since I began working to feed the flock. There are many more people around the world who are doing great work where it's needed most. These people are putting their beliefs into action, and I believe they are not only benefiting their communities but are also taking strides to help heal our world.

Pass On the Good News

If my own journey to feed the world has taught me anything, it's that there are so many opportunities for you to help your larger human family. I'd like to encourage you to reflect peacefully on what else you can do, particularly when it comes to relieving physical hunger.

Remember, these actions will also reinforce for your children the importance of feeding the world. You don't need to be a pro to come up with a way you can offer relief to a member of your human family in need. The beautiful thing is that everyone can do something.

> ►€ FOOD FOR THOUGHT
> ### A Supper Hero's Special Calling
> As a supper hero, there is one special way you help feed the world: by the lessons you teach your children. Family dinners are the stage for teaching life's most important lessons. One of those lessons has to be how your children can contribute to our international human family. Don't let this important lesson go unlearned.

EXERCISES

1. Pass it on.

   What can you do with your family to help pass on the important lesson of feeding the world? Make a list of several potential lessons and review them with your spouse or meal partner. Then make a plan of when you can carry one of those lessons out with your family.

2. Reflect on your role.

   What else can you do to help feed our larger human family? It doesn't have to be anything huge. Take some time to reflect on your capabilities and resources. Decide what you can do to help. Then do what most people don't do when they think about a potential solution to a problem: actually do the thing you think of!

3. Remember our big human family—with a sandwich.

In traveling the world, I discovered a universal meal we all have in common: the sandwich! Remember our big human family as you make a World Chicken Burrito, which includes elements from several cultures. See the recipe on page 136.

A SUPPER HERO'S FAVORITE
⚡ RECIPES ⚡

Crock-Pot Macaroni and Cheese

4 TO 6 SERVINGS

Raising a family is like a long, slow Crock-Pot meal. This Crock-pot comfort-food recipe encourages family collaboration and togetherness. Simply have everyone in the family choose a different ingredient. Maybe someone wants to add bacon or broccoli—throw it all in together! No matter what combination your family comes up with, it will be delicious—mainly because of all the cheese!

Ingredients

2 tablespoons butter

½ white onion, diced

2 tablespoons flour

3 cups uncooked elbow macaroni

8 ounces shredded cheddar cheese

8 ounces shredded pepper jack cheese

1 cup shredded Parmesan cheese

6 cups milk

½ cup white wine

2 teaspoons salt

½ teaspoon white pepper

½ teaspoon garlic powder

Directions

1. Melt the butter in a small pan over medium heat.
2. Add the onion and cook for 3 to 4 minutes until translucent, stirring often.
3. Add the flour to the pan and mix thoroughly; then cook for 2 minutes on low heat.
4. Remove the mixture from the heat and transfer it to a large Crock-Pot.
5. Add 2 cups of milk, and whisk until the flour mixture is completely integrated into the milk.
6. Add the macaroni, cheeses, remaining milk, wine, salt, garlic, and pepper. Mix well. (Optional: add any precooked meats or vegetables.)
7. Cover and cook on high for 2 hours, stirring after an hour.

CRUSTY MAC AND CHEESE: For a crispy, crusty top, transfer the finished macaroni and cheese to a baking dish and top with breadcrumbs. Bake at 425 degrees for 6 to 8 minutes or until golden brown.

Skewers

4 TO 6 SERVINGS

Test how well your family members know each other's "flavors." Create this dish together by putting everyone's name into a hat and having each person draw a name of someone to create a skewer for. There are sweet, salty, bitter, and sour options. Have each person use what he knows to create the perfect skewer for the person whose name he picked!

Ingredients

2 large chicken breasts, cut into 1-inch cubes

1 zucchini, cut into 1-inch cubes

10 medium button mushrooms

1 red onion, quartered and separated

1 bell pepper, seeds and stem removed, cut into 1-inch squares

10 to 12 shrimp, peeled and deveined

2 or 3 Italian sausage links, cut into 1-inch pieces

1 orange, juice and zest

1 clove garlic, minced

2 tablespoons honey

1 tablespoon soy sauce

1 tablespoon chopped fresh herbs (any aromatic herbs, such as rosemary, thyme, or oregano)

¼ cup olive oil

1 tablespoon salt

1 teaspoon black pepper

Directions

1. In a small mixing bowl, create the marinade by combining the orange juice and zest, garlic, honey, soy sauce, fresh herbs, olive oil, salt, and pepper, and mixing well.
2. Place the chicken and shrimp into separate small containers and coat with the marinade.
3. Allow the meats to marinate for at least 2 hours, overnight preferred.
4. Assemble the skewers by alternating meats and vegetables.
5. Spray the assembled skewers with nonstick spray, and season with salt and pepper.
6. Grill the skewers until the meats are cooked through.

TIPS

- Shrimp cooks faster than chicken and sausage, so be careful with your timing.
- Make sure all ingredients are similarly sized to help them cook evenly.
- Soak the skewers in water for an hour before assembling to help prevent burning.

East and West Pasta

This recipe saves you time by creating two distinct dishes with the same pound of precooked spaghetti. The "East" dish is Asian, and the "West" dish is Italian.

East Pasta

3 TO 4 SERVINGS

Ingredients

2 teaspoons sesame oil

¼ onion, julienned

1 clove garlic, minced

5 or 6 basil leaves, chiffonade

1½ tablespoons soy sauce

1 teaspoon fish sauce

1 teaspoon rice wine vinegar

½ cup coconut cream

½ pound spaghetti, cooked

½ pound chicken, cooked and cut into strips

Directions

1. Add the sesame oil to a medium sauté pan, and heat it over medium heat.
2. Once hot, add the onions and cook for 2 minutes, stirring often.
3. Add the garlic and basil, and cook for 1 minute, stirring often.
4. In a separate bowl mix together the soy sauce, fish sauce, vinegar, and coconut cream. Add the liquid mixture into the pan, and reduce the heat to low.
5. Add the spaghetti and chicken and toss well.
6. Once the pasta and chicken are heated and the sauce has reduced (about 5 minutes) remove from the heat and arrange on a plate. Garnish with a few whole basil leaves.

CHIFFONADE: This refers to shredded or finely cut leaf vegetables. To chiffonade the basil, stack the leaves and gently roll them. Then slice the roll to create thin strips.

West Pasta

3 TO 4 SERVINGS

Ingredients

2 tablespoons olive oil

¼ onion, julienned

1 pint cherry tomatoes, halved

1 clove garlic, minced

5 or 6 basil leaves, chiffonade

2 teaspoons salt

1 teaspoon black pepper

½ pound spaghetti, cooked

½ pound chicken, cooked and cut into strips

2 tablespoons chopped parsley

¼ cup shredded Parmesan

Directions

1. Add the olive oil to a medium sauté pan, and heat it over medium heat.
2. Once hot, add the onions, and cook for 2 minutes, stirring often.
3. Add the tomatoes, garlic, and basil, and cook for another 2 minutes, stirring often.
4. Add the salt, pepper, spaghetti, and chicken.
5. Reduce the heat to low, and cook for 5 minutes or until the pasta and chicken are heated.
6. Remove from the heat, and arrange on a plate. Sprinkle with parsley and Parmesan.

PREPARE YOUR PRECOOKED PASTA: Precooked pasta can taste almost fresh! Start by cooking the pasta al dente. Next, run it under cold water to stop the cooking process, and toss it with olive oil before storing it covered in the fridge.

Eggs Three Ways

Here are three egg recipes to help you get started with family meals. Make it easy with Egg in a Nest or a little more complicated with a scallion omelet, or pour your eggs into a crust to make a quiche!

Egg in a Nest
1 SERVING

Ingredients

1 tablespoon butter

1 slice of bread

1 egg

1 slice of cheese

Directions

1. Melt the butter in a small nonstick pan over medium heat.
2. Using a drinking glass, or a round object of a similar size, cut the center out of the slice of bread, and place both pieces in the heated pan.
3. Crack the egg into the hole in the bread slice.
4. Once the bread is toasted and the egg is mostly cooked, flip the bread and the egg over, and top with cheese.
5. When the egg is cooked to your liking and the cheese is melted remove from the heat and serve.

MAKE IT A MEAL: For a complete meal, add ham or precooked bacon before topping with the cheese. You can also make the dish fancy by adding crispy pancetta, arugula, and reduced balsamic vinegar.

Scallion Omelet

4 SERVINGS

Ingredients

2 tablespoons olive oil

6 eggs

3 tablespoons water

1 teaspoon salt

1 teaspoon black pepper

¼ cup scallion, cut thinly on a bias

Directions

1. Heat the oil in a medium nonstick pan over medium-high heat.
2. Crack the eggs into a medium bowl and beat well with a fork until fluffy.
3. Add the water, salt, pepper, and scallions to the eggs, and mix well.
4. Add the egg mixture to the heated pan.
5. Once halfway cooked, lift the sides of the omelet and let any raw egg run underneath and continue cooking.
6. When most of the egg is cooked and becomes fluffy, use a spatula to flip the omelet carefully to avoid splashing any hot oil.
7. Cook through, remove from the heat, and serve.

Quiche

6 SERVINGS

Crust Ingredients

1½ cups flour (plus 3 tablespoons flour for the table)

½ teaspoon salt

8 tablespoons cold butter, cut into small cubes

2 tablespoons cold water

Filling Ingredients

6 eggs

¼ cup onion, diced

2 teaspoons fresh thyme, chopped

½ cup milk

1 tablespoon salt

1 teaspoon black pepper

2 links cooked sausage, cut into ½-inch pieces

½ cup Gruyère cheese, shredded

Directions for the Crust

1. Mix the flour and salt thoroughly in a medium mixing bowl.
2. Add the butter to the flour, and mix in using your fingers until it is completely integrated and mealy (with a sand-like texture).
3. Add the water, and knead until a dough forms, about 2 minutes. Avoid overkneading.
4. Place the dough on a well-floured surface, and roll it out into an 11-inch circle.
5. Move the rolled-out dough into a 9-inch pie or tart pan, and trim the edges.
6. Press all the edges of the dough with the tines of a fork to make small ridges.
7. Use a fork to poke holes (about 30 pokes) in the bottom of the crust to avoid bubbling.
8. Transfer the crust into the refrigerator to rest for 20 minutes, and preheat the oven to 375 degrees.
9. Once rested, bake for 20 minutes.

Directions for the Filling

1. Combine the eggs, thyme, milk, salt, and pepper in a large mixing bowl, and beat with a fork until fluffy.
2. Spread the onions, the sausage, and half of the cheese in the prebaked crust.
3. Pour the egg mixture into the crust, and add the remaining cheese.
4. Bake at 375 degrees for 30 minutes or until set. Insert a toothpick or a sharp knife into the center and then remove. If it comes out clean, the quiche is done. If it comes out wet, continue baking.

TIPS

- You can make the crust dough in a food processor, using the plastic blade.
- Try not to overwork the dough, or it will become tough.
- Add your favorite vegetables to the quiche.

Carrots for Everyone

This recipe helps you connect with your children by having everyone eat the same thing! First, fix your little ones home-made carrot baby food. Then elevate that baby food into one of two delicious dishes: roasted carrots or carrot bisque.

Puréed Carrots
4 TO 5 SERVINGS

Ingredients

1½ cups carrot, peeled and cut into medium-size chunks

¼ teaspoon salt
2 to 3 tablespoons water

Directions

1. Steam the carrots until soft and tender.
2. Transfer to a food processer and add salt.
3. Blend until smooth.

❓ **DID YOU KNOW?** Consistency matters. You can adjust the baby food you make to suit your children's preferences. Typically, children like the food to be thicker as they get older.

Roasted Carrots

4 SERVINGS

Ingredients

1 tablespoon olive oil

2 cloves garlic, minced

2 teaspoons salt

½ teaspoon black pepper

½ teaspoon Italian seasoning

¼ teaspoon marjoram

2 pinches allspice

2 tablespoons brown sugar

3 cups carrot (about 1½ pounds), peeled and cut into bite-size pieces

Directions

1. In a small mixing bowl, combine all the ingredients except for the carrots, and mix well.
2. Add the carrots and toss until evenly coated.
3. Place the coated carrots in a baking dish, and roast at 450 degrees for 25 minutes or until tender and well caramelized.

TIP: Line the baking dish with foil for easy cleanup.

Carrot Bisque

2 SERVINGS

Ingredients

2 tablespoons butter

½ cup onion, diced

3 cups carrots (about 1½ pounds), peeled
and cut into medium-size pieces

1 clove garlic, chopped

3 cups chicken stock

2 teaspoons salt

½ teaspoon white pepper

1 teaspoon ground ginger

¼ cup Pinot Grigio

¼ cup heavy cream

Directions

1. Melt the butter in a medium pot over medium heat.
2. Add the onions and cook for 3 minutes.
3. Add the carrots and garlic and cook for 3 minutes, stirring frequently.
4. Add the chicken stock, salt, pepper, ginger, and wine, and simmer until tender, about 15 minutes.
5. Puree with a food processor, a blender, or an immersion blender.
6. Remove from the heat, add the cream and mix thoroughly.

TIPS

- Garnish the bisque with croutons, fresh herbs, or a dollop of crème fraîche.
- Make large batches of bisque and freeze in quart-size ziplock bags for future meals.
- Serve with a glass of Pinot Grigio.

Chicken Tenders with a Bonus Lunch

This meal is designed to help you get your teen involved in meals! Not only can they help you make these delicious chicken tenders, but they can use the leftovers to make themselves a healthy salad to take to school for lunch. I've also included some fun salad dressing recipes to let them practice making their own dressing and allow them to customize their salads.

Chicken Tenders
2 SERVINGS

Ingredients

2 pounds chicken tenders (or chicken breasts cut into 2-inch strips)

2 cups buttermilk

½ cup hot sauce

2 teaspoons black pepper (for marinade)

2 cups vegetable oil

1½ cups flour

1½ cups Italian seasoned bread crumbs

1 tablespoon Old Bay seasoning

1 tablespoon cornstarch

1 teaspoon salt

½ teaspoon black pepper (for flour)

Directions

1. Place chicken, buttermilk, hot sauce, and pepper into a gallon-size ziplock bag, and let it marinate overnight in the refrigerator.
2. Heat the oil in a large pan (cast iron is ideal) over medium heat.
3. Combine the flour, bread crumbs, Old Bay seasoning, cornstarch, salt, and pepper in a medium bowl.
4. Place the marinated chicken in the bowl with the flour, and dredge it until it is completely covered with the breading. Discard the marinade and excess flour.
5. Carefully place the dredged chicken in the heated oil. Be sure not to overcrowd the pan, or the tenders will become soggy. You may have to cook the chicken in batches.

If this is the case, use a slotted spoon to remove debris and let the oil reheat to the proper temperature between batches.

6. Cook the tenders until they are golden brown on each side and their internal temperature reaches 165, about 3 to 4 minutes on each side. (For thicker tenders, you may have to bake them at 375 degrees for a few minutes to ensure doneness.)

7. Once cooked, transfer the tenders to a sheet pan with a cooling rack or a paper towel to allow any excess oil to drip off.

CAUTION: Raw chicken may contain harmful salmonella-causing bacteria. It is important to clean and sanitize all utensils and surfaces that come in contact with raw chicken.

REHEAT TENDERS IN THE OVEN: You can reheat fried tenders by baking them at 375 degrees for 8 minutes.

Chicken Tender Salad
BONUS LUNCH

Ingredients

Lettuce and desired vegetables

2 leftover chicken tenders, cut into strips

Salad dressing (see optional dressing recipes that follow)

Directions

1. Pour the desired amount of dressing into a Tupperware container, and top with lettuce, chicken tender strips, and your choice of toppings. Cover.

2. When ready to eat, shake the container to coat everything with the dressing.

Honey Mustard Dressing

¼ cup yellow mustard

¼ cup honey

pinch salt

pinch black pepper

pinch garlic powder

Combine all the ingredients in a small bowl and mix until well blended.

Honey Mustard Vinaigrette Dressing

¼ cup yellow mustard

¼ cup honey

pinch salt

pinch black pepper

pinch garlic powder

2 teaspoons red wine vinegar

2 teaspoons extra virgin olive oil

1. Combine mustard, honey, salt, pepper, and garlic powder in a small bowl and mix until well blended.
2. Add vinegar until well blended. Slowly drizzle the olive oil into the honey-mustard mixture while whisking until emulsified (when all the oil has been integrated).

Thousand Island Dressing

1 tablespoon chopped dill pickle

2 teaspoons pickle juice

¼ cup mayonnaise

3 tablespoons ketchup

¼ teaspoon salt

¼ teaspoon garlic powder

Combine all the ingredients in small bowl and mix until well blended.

Ranch Dressing

¼ cup mayonnaise

¼ cup sour cream

½ teaspoon garlic powder

½ teaspoon onion powder

½ teaspoon salt

2 teaspoon apple cider vinegar

2 tablespoons buttermilk

Combine all the ingredients in small mixing bowl and mix until well blended.

MAKE A RANCH VINAIGRETTE: It's easy to transform this ranch recipe into a vinaigrette. Simply take ½ cup of the prepared dressing, add 2 teaspoons of balsamic vinegar, and stir until well blended. Next, slowly drizzle in 2 teaspoons of olive oil, and whisk until all of the oil has been integrated.

Thirst-Quenching Shrimp Dishes

Here are some dishes to enjoy for young adults' meals at home. These recipes also incorporate ingredients many young adults enjoy: wine and beer! You can use these recipes to explore how different adult beverages can complement a meal.

Shrimp Scampi
4 TO 6 SERVINGS

Ingredients

1 tablespoon butter
¼ cup shallots, chopped
1 pound shrimp, peeled, and deveined
3 cloves garlic, chopped
1 cup sauvignon blanc wine
2 cups cream

2 teaspoons salt
1 teaspoon white pepper
1 tablespoon fresh parsley, chopped
½ pound linguine, cooked (reserve 1 cup pasta water before draining)
½ cup grated Parmesan

Directions

1. Melt the butter in a large pan over medium heat.
2. Add the shallots and cook for 3 minutes.
3. Add the shrimp and cook until the shrimp is pink and firm and the tail turns red, stirring frequently.
4. Remove the shrimp and reserve for later.
5. Add the garlic, wine, cream, salt, and pepper and simmer until thickened.
6. Add parsley, shrimp, and linguine, and toss to coat. If the sauce is too thick, add a few tablespoons of the reserved pasta water to thin to your desired consistency.
7. Remove from the heat and arrange on plates. Finish with grated Parmesan.

TIP: Remove the shrimp tails before cooking so the dish is easier to eat.

Beer Shrimp Scampi
4 TO 6 SERVINGS

Ingredients

4 tablespoons butter, cut into cubes

1 pound shrimp, peeled, and deveined

1 cup flour

1 teaspoon cornstarch

1 tablespoon salt

2 teaspoons black pepper

3 cloves garlic, minced

12-ounce can beer

2 teaspoons Old Bay or creole seasoning

1½ tablespoons chives or parsley, chopped

2 cups rice, cooked

Directions

1. Melt half of the butter in a medium pan over medium heat.
2. Mix the flour, cornstarch, salt, and pepper in a small bowl.
3. Toss the shrimp with the flour mixture until the shrimp is completely covered; then shake off the excess flour and add the shrimp to the pan.
4. Cook the shrimp until pink and firm; then remove from the pan and reserve for later.
5. Add the garlic and cook for 1 minute, stirring frequently.
6. Add the beer and the seafood seasoning, and scrape any caramelized food from the bottom of the pan with a whisk or a spoon to release more flavor. Simmer until slightly reduced, about 5 minutes.
7. Turn off the heat and add the shrimp, chives, and remaining butter.
8. Mix the sauce until the butter is incorporated. Serve over rice.

TIP: Different beers will give the dish different flavors. Any light or amber beer works well. Avoid darker or heavily flavored beers.

Three-in-One Beef

Many parents struggle to cook for just two people again after their children leave home. These recipes use a single package of economically priced cubed steak to make three delicious one-pan meals! This should help you adjust to cooking smaller meals. They are also great meals to teach the young adults in your life as they start making meals on their own.

Philly-Pino Steak Sandwich

2 SERVINGS

Ingredients

⅓ pound stew meat, pounded flat
1 teaspoon salt
½ teaspoon black pepper
¼ teaspoon garlic powder
2 teaspoons olive oil

¼ onion, julienned
3 mushrooms, sliced
1 tablespoon mayonnaise
2 slices American cheese
1 hoagie roll

Directions

1. Melt the butter in a medium sauté pan over medium heat.
2. Place the steak on a large piece of plastic wrap, fold the wrap over it, and pound the beef flat with a meat mallet, being careful not to tear the beef.
3. Season the flattened beef with half of the salt, pepper, and garlic. Place the seasoned beef in the hot pan and brown on each side.
4. Remove the beef from the pan and set aside to rest. While the steak is resting, add the onions, mushrooms, and remaining salt, pepper and garlic to the hot pan and cook for 4 minutes, stirring occasionally.

5. Move the vegetables to one side of the pan and place the split roll on the other side and gently toast. Remove the toasted roll and spread with the mayonnaise.
6. Place the beef in the pan and top with the vegetables and cheese, and allow it to melt. Transfer the filling to the roll with a large spatula.

NO MEAT MALLET? If you don't have a meat mallet, try using a small sauté pan to pound the steak flat.

Stir-Fry

2 SERVINGS

Ingredients

1 tablespoon butter

⅓ pound stew meat, cut into thin strips

1 teaspoon salt

½ teaspoon black pepper

½ teaspoon garlic powder

1 pinch cinnamon

¼ teaspoon paprika

¼ onion, julienned

4 or 5 button mushrooms, quartered

2 teaspoons soy sauce

1 pinch crushed red pepper

1 teaspoon red wine vinegar

1 cup cooked rice

1 teaspoon chopped cilantro

Directions

1. Melt the butter in a medium sauté pan over medium-high heat.
2. Add the beef to the hot pan along with the salt, pepper, garlic, cinnamon, and paprika, and brown the beef slightly.
3. Add the onions and mushrooms, and cook for 2 to 3 minutes, stirring occasionally.
4. Add the soy sauce, crushed red pepper, and vinegar, and cook for another 2 to 3 minutes.
5. Remove from the heat and serve over the cooked rice. Top with the fresh cilantro.

Beef Bourguignon

2 SERVINGS

Ingredients

2 teaspoons olive oil

⅓ pound stew meat

1 tablespoon salt

1 teaspoon black pepper

2 tablespoons flour

½ large onion, diced

3 small carrots, peeled and large-diced

4 medium button mushrooms, halved

2 cloves garlic, chopped

1 cup red wine

2 cups beef broth

1 tablespoon ketchup

2 teaspoons Italian seasoning

2 bay leaves

Directions

1. Heat the olive oil in a small saucepan over medium heat.
2. Season the beef with half of the salt and pepper; then toss in the flour.
3. Shake off any excess flour and add the seasoned meat to the hot pan.
4. Brown the meat on all sides; then add the onion, carrots, mushrooms, and garlic, and cook for 3 minutes, stirring occasionally.
5. Add the remaining ingredients and reduce the heat to low.
6. Simmer until the sauce has thickened to a stew-like consistency and the vegetables are cooked through and tender, about 30 minutes.
7. Remove from the heat and remove the bay leaves.

NOTE: Always remember to remove the bay leaves before serving the stew. They impart lots of flavor to the Beef Bourguignon but are inedible.

STEW BROTH THIN? If the stew broth is not thick enough but the vegetables are tender, coat a teaspoon of butter with flour and add it to the stew. Whisk well, and the broth should thicken.

Bourbon Salmon for Two
2 SERVINGS

Here is a special meal from my book *Spicing Up Married Life* that you and your spouse should try when you become empty nesters. The salmon is nutritious and delicious, and the youthful Kentucky bourbon glaze will spice up your meal!

Ingredients

¼ cup bourbon

¼ cup honey

1 orange, zest and juice

1 teaspoon salt

½ teaspoon cayenne

2 salmon fillets, 6 to 8 ounces each, skin removed

WARNING: Use caution when you cook with alcohol. Have a lid handy to extinguish any flareups.

Directions

1. Combine the bourbon, honey, orange zest, and orange juice in a small saucepan over medium-low heat. Cook until thickened enough to coat the back of a spoon, about 10 minutes.
2. Remove the sauce from the heat and allow it to cool to room temperature.
3. Season all sides of the salmon with salt and cayenne.
4. Place the salmon on a rack placed on a sheet pan. Drizzle half of the cooled glaze on the salmon to cover the top.
5. Bake the salmon at 350 for about 10 minutes.
6. Baste the salmon with the remaining glaze and continue to bake to your desired doneness, 15 to 20 minutes total.
7. Remove the salmon from the heat and let it rest for 5 minutes.

TIP: Lining your baking sheet with foil makes cleanup a breeze! Baking on a rack encourages air flow around the salmon and ensures more even cooking.

Mushroom Risotto and Chocolate Rice Porridge

Mushrom risotto is elegant, delicious and edible by family members who need softer foods — the perfect recipe for an intergenerational meal! Plus, everyone from Grandma down to the youngest at the table will love the delicious chocolate rice porridge — a Philippine tradition!

Mushroom Risotto
4 TO 6 SIDE-DISH SERVINGS

Ingredients

2 tablespoons butter

¼ cup shallot or white onion, diced finely

1½ cups chopped mushrooms

1 cup Arborio rice (preferred because of its high starch content)

1 clove garlic, minced

1 cup white wine

4 cups chicken broth, warm

1 teaspoon black pepper

2 teaspoons salt

½ cup Parmesan cheese, shredded

2 tablespoons fresh herbs, chopped (rosemary, thyme, or parsley, or any combination of them)

Directions

1. Melt the butter in a medium pan over medium heat.
2. Add the onion and mushrooms to the heated pan. Cook for 3 minutes, stirring frequently.
3. Add the rice and toast for 2 minutes, stirring frequently.
4. Add the garlic and wine, reduce heat to low, and cook until the wine is absorbed.
5. Add 2 cups of warm chicken broth, and cook until absorbed, stirring occasionally.

6. Once the broth is absorbed, add additional broth, a ladle at a time, until the rice is cooked through and softened. Use warm water or additional broth if needed.
7. Once the rice is fully cooked, remove it from the heat, and add the salt, pepper, cheese, and herbs. Mix well.

TIP: Use warm stock. Adding cold liquids always slows the cooking process, which can make the rice cook unevenly.

Chocolate Rice Porridge

3 TO 4 SERVINGS

Ingredients

2 tablespoons butter

1 cup rice

1 quart milk

2 cups water

¼ cup cocoa powder

¾ cup sugar

1 teaspoon salt

Directions

1. Melt the butter in a medium pan over low heat.
2. Add the rice to the heated pan and toast for 5 minutes, stirring frequently.
3. While the rice is toasting, combine the milk, water, cocoa, sugar, and salt in a medium saucepot over low heat, whisking until everything is dissolved.
4. Add half of the milk mixture to the toasted rice, and cook until it is absorbed, stirring occasionally.
5. Add the rest of the milk mixture, and cook, stirring occasionally, until the liquid is absorbed and the rice is tender and creamy. If more liquid is needed, use warm water.

TIP: Add additional layers of flavor. Try adding chopped nuts or dried fruits to the chocolate porridge after cooking for even more yum!

Chocolate Mousse with Spicy Streusel
4 TO 6 SERVINGS

Family life isn't always sweet. Very often we face challenges and we may even need to turn up the heat to tackle difficult issues—but we can't let the heat overpower us. This dessert is the same way! It uses heat to complement a semisweet chocolate mousse.

Mousse Ingredients

16 ounces dark chocolate, chopped

2 tablespoons Grand Marnier

4 eggs, separated

1 quart heavy whipping cream

⅛ teaspoon cream of tartar

1 batch streusel (see the recipe below)

1 bunch fresh mint leaves for garnish

Optional: zest and juice of one orange

Directions for the Mousse

1. In a double boiler, melt the chocolate with Grand Marnier and the zest and juice of one orange (if using).
2. Temper 4 egg yolks and add to the chocolate. Make sure the chocolate is not so hot that it cooks the eggs. Whisk together and set aside to cool.
3. In a chilled bowl, use a hand blender to whip the cream until soft peaks form. Set aside, and reserve some for topping.
4. In a separate clean bowl, add the cream of tartar to the egg whites, and whip until soft peaks form. The cream of tartar helps to stabilize and stiffen the egg whites.
5. Gently fold (*do not* mix) the melted chocolate into the egg whites until the color is consistent. Gently fold the mixture of chocolate and egg white with the whipped cream until it is a uniform color.
6. Put it in the refrigerator to chill and firm up before serving.
7. To serve: sprinkle a layer of streusel on the bottom of a cup, spoon in some mousse, and then top with more streusel. Finish with a dollop of whipped cream and a sprig of fresh mint.

CLEAN IS KEY: Be sure to use a clean bowl and to clean the mixer thoroughly before whipping the egg whites. Otherwise, any fat from the cream or the egg yolks will prevent the egg whites from stiffening.

Streusel Ingredients

3 cups panko bread crumbs

1 cup butter, melted

2 teaspoons cinnamon

1 teaspoon allspice

¼ cup brown sugar

½ teaspoon salt

2 teaspoons cayenne

Directions

1. Preheat the oven to 375 degrees.
2. Combine all the ingredients in a large mixing bowl and mix well.
3. Transfer the mixture to a baking pan and bake for 12 minutes, stirring halfway through, or until toasted to golden brown.
4. Remove from the oven and allow to come to room temperature.

World Chicken Burritos

2 SERVINGS

The sandwich is a universal meal we all have in common. This one combines elements from several cultures. It's a reminder that we are all one big human family—a life lesson that is as easy to take away as the sandwich itself!

Avocado Spread Ingredients

1 ripe avocado, seed and skin removed
1 tablespoon extra virgin olive oil
¼ teaspoon cumin

½ teaspoon salt
¼ teaspoon black pepper
juice of ½ lime

Directions for the Avocado Spread

1. Mix all the ingredients in a small bowl with a fork or a whisk until smooth.
2. Cover with plastic wrap until ready to serve.

Burrito Ingredients

large tortillas
1 pound chicken, cooked and shredded or sliced
1 batch avocado spread (see the recipe above)

½ cup black beans, heated
¼ cup shredded cheddar cheese
¼ cup red onion, diced
2 tablespoons cilantro, chopped

Directions for the Burritos

1. Heat the tortillas in the oven or directly on the flame on the stovetop until warm and slightly toasted. Lay the heated tortillas on a clean surface.
2. Spread 2 tablespoons of avocado spread over each tortilla, leaving 1 inch of the tortilla uncovered around the edge.

3. Top each tortilla with half of the remaining ingredients.
4. Fold the side of the tortilla closest to you to the middle, over the filling. Then fold the left and right sides of the tortilla 1 to 2 inches toward the middle. Finally, roll the stuffed tortilla away from you to form a tight cylinder.

TIP: The avocado will turn brown quickly, so try to prepare the burritos as close to mealtime as possible.

ABOUT THE AUTHOR

Fr. Leo E. Patalinghug is a member of a community of consecrated life, Voluntas Dei (The Will of God). He is the founder, host, and director of Plating Grace, an international food-and-faith movement to inspire families to gather around the dinner table, and is the chairman of the non-profit group The Table Foundation. He is the host of EWTN's TV show *Savoring Our Faith*, the radio show *Entertaining Truth*, and the podcast *Shoot the Shiitake with Father Leo*. He is a best-selling author and internationally renown conference speaker. His experiences and perspectives have reached a vast audience beyond church walls, especially with his victory on the Food Network competition Throwdown with Bobby Flay. His approach to pastoral ministry and his teachings on the Theology of Food and pastoral care have helped countless families to reconnect and to do the important work of feeding one another.

Sophia Institute